Chasing the Dragon's Tail

Chasing the Dragon's Tail:
Finding Passion In Your Purpose

Craig Fullerton

atmosphere press

To my wife Sue and daughter Hannah. My parents Ron and Val - thank you for your support and willingness to listen; for without that, this book would never have manifested and would have forever remained a journal of passionate ideas and notebook scratchings.

CONTENTS

Part 1 – Values and Motivation

Part 2 – Passion

Part 3 – Certainty and Decisiveness

Part 4 – Mindset and Modelling

ACKNOWLEDGEMENTS

"Your time is limited, so don't waste it living someone else's life. Don't be trapped by dogma - which is living with the results of other people's thinking. Don't let the noise of others' opinions drown out your own inner voice. And most important, have the courage to follow your heart and intuition." - Steve Jobs

While the insights for this book happened in a flash, the research, planning, starting, stopping, reflecting, and restarting was an ongoing journey. The passion to want to write it and the purpose to actually write and publish it took 8 years from conception to completion. It was certainly an incredible journey through experiences, stories, and reflection of my own life with some challenges along the way, nevertheless I am thankfully expanded due to them.

I was helped along the way by many and I am sincerely grateful for their advice, encouragement, and the odd joke to break me out of procrastination mode. I especially wish to thank those of you that supported me when I decided to go live and seek out publishers. This helped me to decide if I was on a good thing or not. Colleagues, friends, and past students from across the globe; through their silent shout-out to their friends, social media, and networks, they sang their support for me. Sincere thank you for keeping it real. China crew- Donita, Richard, Kim and Kendal. Norway/USA friends - Peggy, Melinda, Karl, and my Aussie mates, Rik, Emma and Len, who put their trust in me and this book before it was written. Thank you.

My mentors and coaches for keeping me on track, encouraging and advising me along the journey. Particularly my coaching cheer squad Rik Schnabel , Dr Justin Kennedy, and Gordana Kennedy for reminding me why I should do this and for balancing me. A special thanks to Rik and Justin for each contributing a foreword for this book and their faith in me and my message. I am humbly grateful. A special thanks to my first coach and trainer that introduced me to various aspects of NLP training and accelerated learning; who started me on this incredible journey of discovery - Christopher Howard.

My editor, Phillip Pantuso, for challenging the Writer in me to allow the reader to gain the most from this book, Nick Courtright and my publishing team at Atmosphere Press for being enthusiastic in reaching out to identify the potential of my message in this book and publish. Tom Pagliaro and the team from Publishizer for giving me the opportunity to keep it real and providing a platform for me to share the Chasing the Dragon's Tail message.

I am most grateful to my wife Susan and daughter Hannah for allowing me the space for my passion to write this and the many late nights. Thank you too to my dear family, Mum and Dad, Scott and Debbie for listening to my ideas, rants, and vision over the years and giving me a reality check when needed.

Thank you to my fellow coaches, neuroscience, education, and NLP friends; the many colleagues and students for your hearts and minds that allowed a sounding board for these concepts over the years as your coach, teacher and colleague.

Thank you.

Craig

Foreword (i)
By Rik Schnabel

When I think of who would be the best person to write this book, there is no one other than Craig Fullerton who comes to mind. Craig is one of my special and select mentees. He is a committed, talented Coach, and also a good friend. He is a success in his own right, and it is truly an honour to be asked to write his foreword.

For 18 wonderful years as a 'Brain Untrainer,' I've been transforming people's lives by changing how they think. There are a handful of us doing this work. Craig is another with this gift. We know that just one new idea; one new neural pathway can take a person's life from poverty to riches and from depression to joy. We know how to frame opportunity and are fully aware that our words have power. There is nothing we love more than witnessing a magical shift in a person's life.

My love of transformational linguistics had me write five best-selling books and I know great work when I see it. This book is exceptional, transformative, and insightful. You now have gold in your hands. More so, should you act on what you read among the prosperous prose, you will save yourself years of pain and heartache, and avoid the inevitable tears of trial and error. Craig knows how to use his words in life shifting ways. He knows them better than most and will guide you well.

Smart people read, learn, and follow the tail of the dragon; those rare few who are living extraordinary lives. While others chase their own tail or buy into other people's limited beliefs. They run in circles by following the advice of people who have one thing they don't –

they've just lived longer. That's all. Age does not guarantee wisdom. Too many follow bad, age-old advice; the tales that comes from people we know, but don't admire. A huge mistake and a huge cost to progress.

Chasing the Dragon's Tail solves one of the greatest problems that every school leaver and graduate faces; the answers to three questions. The first question: *Who am I?* The second question: *What is my purpose?* The third seeks the fast track or the high road: *Which is my path?* It is one thing to get the answer to these questions wrong. It is a violation to life itself to not attempt to answer them at all. Sadly, the masses take those three unanswered questions to their graves. You, however, will be enlightened by reading on.

Every success story has answered those three life-defining questions and ignited the dragon's flame from within. Those who have found success don't need deadlines. They rarely require inspiration. They are self-motivated because they engineered their own internal furnace – a dragon's flame that will never die.

What burns me up, however, is that up to 90 percent of book buyers want success; they have good intentions but seldom read beyond the first chapter. An opportunity is in their hands and yet, it never reaches their heads. You can now decide to join the top 10 percent by merely reading the entire book. I promise, you *will* be rewarded. Success is easier than you think once you realise that most people quit on themselves. You don't have to win at anything. You just have to stay in the game.

Chasing the Dragon's Tail will teach you how to ignite your breath. It will give you the match, the scratch, and the fuel. It is for this reason that you must finish this book and act on Craig's most worthy advice.

Chinese dragons symbolise potent and auspicious powers. They are lucky and strong. You need to know that this book is deeply fortunate and prosperous. It is one of the best books I have ever read on finding your purpose. I know you will gain much from it. Appropriately, your book commences from "The Dragon's Heart" because everything that is truly great starts there. I hope you enjoy it as much as I did.

Rik Schnabel
Australia's #1
Brain Untrainer
www.LifeBeyondLimits.com.au

Foreword (ii)
By Dr. Justin James Kennedy

"It's all about how we feel, not what we think that makes all the difference." -Craig Fullerton

Drawing from diverse fields of applied neuroscience and cognitive psychology, Craig crosses the traditional boundaries and theories that have separated scientific thinking and human experience in the past. In doing so he opens the door to a bold new paradigm of self-discovery and empowerment - a way of thinking and living based upon what is possible in our lives.

He discusses what we accept as scientific facts, leading us on an engaging and fun step-by-step journey to achieving our greatest potential.

Craig has helped numerous people across 5 continents and over 2000 hours of coaching, training and teaching to transform their lives and their businesses through his workshops, Speaking, executive and personal coaching. He's been fortunate enough to work with leaders, managers, CEO's, teacher-leaders and students.

Many books present theories of success, and are focused on specific things such as business, life skills, relationships and so on. *Chasing the Dragon's Tail* is an easy to understand guide and collection of tools, with real-life example for gaining clarity on your life's purpose.

This is not just theories. This book strips back the best of the best and focuses on identifying, the core tools for success and personal development. It is the psychological and neurological framework you can follow to start taking control of your own destiny. Lots of real-life and personal examples with easy to do activities that will give the reader enjoyment, learning and many 'Aha' moments toward success.

Having read and done the activities in this book the reader will have more certainty as to who they are, what are their true feelings and attitudes toward their career, personal development and how to find success and keep it for life. This book will help you become the champion you were always meant to be.

Dr. Justin James Kennedy

Professor of Neuroscience, Executive Coach, Psychologist.

www.professorkennedy.com

Chapter 1
Introduction to Your Journey

"As you think, so shall you become...If you spend too much time thinking about a thing, you'll never get it done. Make at least one definite move daily towards your goal."
 - Bruce Lee *(Little Dragon)*

If I were to help you discover a way to easily improve your mindset, health, and happiness, would it be useful? It is now time to expand the realms of possibility. I will show you how to create your own success, because sometimes you have to experience success first hand to believe it. I certainly have had my fair share of aha moments and learnings throughout my life and continue to do so. What I didn't know was that these moments, these experiences, would help me write this book. Throughout this book, you will read of my experiences and my self-discovery, and the impact these have had on my life, my focus, and purpose.

As you read this book and engage with the activities, the information, and stories, you will discover tools and techniques that will help you unlock your understanding of who you are, why you do what you do, what you need to do to be happy and find success, and your ability to be who you want to be easily and effortlessly, in order to achieve your dreams and your goals. Your life will be transformed forever and you will absolutely understand your passion and purpose. You will take what you will learn to create personal power. The way in which you think will be changed for the better. You are about to grow your awareness and discover more about yourself. For example, your career preferences, personal preferences, moods, and attitudes, to name a few.

Many books on personal development present theories of success and are focused on specific things such as business, life skills, and relationships. In *Chasing the Dragon's Tail,* I present the best of the best - the core elements for achieving success in an inspirational, conversational style within an easy-to-understand guide, and a collection of tools with real-life examples that, when explored and implemented, will help you gain clarity on your life's purpose.

I have synthesized hundreds of resources and thousands of hours throughout my 20+ years spent researching all aspects of personal and professional development, including my experience as an NLP master coach and trainer, executive leadership coach, musician, teacher, education leader, and keynote speaker.

Without being limited to specific vocations or ages, I have focused on helping you find your "passion in your purpose" in a one-of-a-kind resource for everybody - teenager or student, employee, CEO. Anybody who is reflecting on their purpose in their life or striving for success in their job. From my own exploration and comprehensive study of neuroscience, cognitive psychology, and coaching, I strip personal and professional development systems back to the major core elements for you to achieve success.

See some special offers at the end of this book to thank you for taking the time to read and learn from what is included here.

Throughout this book, you will be supported on the journey and you will create new approaches, thinking styles, and techniques for your success. You may have dreams that you aspire to that you haven't achieved yet; happier and healthier goals that you want but don't know why you never achieve them or how to achieve them.

My goal is to share tools and insights so you can achieve your goals, enhance your life, or at least embark on some self-discovery to help you identify your purpose.

To gain the most from this book, be honest with yourself, play full out, reach into your heart. Be challenged and rise to the challenges. Determine how you can take control to evaluate, change, and implement what you need, in order to be who you were meant to be. Swallow your ego, embrace the self-talk, and do the activities. Be happy and confident knowing who you are, your mission, and why it is so. Be brave, step up, commit, and enjoy the journey.

So why *Chasing the Dragon's Tail* as the title? The idea of chasing your tail is to be very busy or working very hard at some task but accomplishing little or nothing as a result; to be engaged in some fruitless or futile task or endeavor. Chasing the dragon's tail is a metaphor for life. If you keep doing what you are doing, you will always be chasing who you are, and not embracing your passion and purpose. In this book, I share tools, techniques, and stories from my own journey to help you avoid doing the same things the same way every day without really knowing who you are, why you are here, or what you are striving for.

Dragons are important creatures in Chinese mythology, folklore, and culture. They traditionally symbolize potency, power, and strength, and are seen as lucky and good.

During the days of Imperial China, the Emperor often

used the dragon as a symbol of his power and strength. In Chinese culture and mythology, the Dragon was the symbolic guardian to the Gods, and was the **source of true wisdom.** The dragon represented two of the ancient elements - Earth and Water, endowing the creature with **powers of illusion and strength**. Shaolin Buddhists saw him as a **vision of enlightened truth.** Chinese Dragons are **symbolic of being lucky**, propitious, powerful, and noble; not as monsters. The Dragon is a **powerful symbol.**

During the Tang dynasty, Emperors wore robes with a dragon motif as an imperial symbol, and high officials might also be presented with dragon robes. In the Yuan dynasty, the two-horned five-clawed dragon was designated for use by the Son of Heaven or Emperor only, while the four-clawed dragon was used by the princes and nobles. Similarly, during the Ming and Qing dynasty, the five-clawed dragon was strictly reserved for use by the Emperor only. The dragon in the Qing dynasty appeared on the first Chinese national flag. The Chinese dragon is a spiritual and cultural symbol that represents prosperity and good luck.

To stop chasing the dragon's tail is to resolve your doubt, know who you are, what you value, what drives you. Determine what is your why and embrace the self-confidence, the power and strength of the dragon, to know your dragon.

> *"Control yourself, let others do what they will.*
> *This does not mean you are weak.*
> *Control your heart, obey the principles of life.*
> *This does not mean others are strong."*
> \-   Southern China Dragon motto

Thank you for your trust! You are about to embark on an incredible journey of self-discovery. You will find your inner dragon, your dragon mind, which you can apply to your life, career, and finances to know yourself and achieve success.

Research shows us that nearly 80% of people are not happy at work[1] because of an internal conflict and values not being lived. They live their work life based on their assumed role; what they think they should do based on what's in their head, rather than living their life to the fullest in their work by embracing a job they enjoy, a job based on their passions and interests. Therefore, they are often not fulfilled in work and/or life. You must focus on the why in order to discover and know your core values. This reflects that it is about how we *feel*, not what we think that makes all the difference. *Chasing the Dragon's Tail* aims to inspire and light your Dragon's Fire from within and to help you determine what is directing you.

The tools, information, exercises, and examples I share with you in this book will help you to create leverage for what you want; to help you to BE who you are and to get clarity on what are your motivational drivers. Motivation is a major game changer to your success. You will learn how to discover these in your career and in your life. For example, when you are confident at work or at play, WHY are you then and not at other times, such as when you address a meeting, interview for that next job, or have that

---

[1] http://www.businessinsider.com/what-do-you-do-when-you-hate-your-job-2010-10
https://www.linkedin.com/pulse/80-people-linkedin-dont-enjoy-hate-job-dan-thomas

conversation?

The tools shared here will help you to become the expert about YOU. If you don't know what you are looking for, you're never going to find it. There is no course on how to find passion or purpose in your work. Have some fun and hit those MAGIC moments as you embark on self-discovery to find your true self, your values, beliefs, and motivators. Your drivers and passions. You likely want to be passionate with what you do in order to express your brilliance and have a positive impact in the world. The information in this book will inspire and implore you to discover and live your story.

I know, I've been there, chasing the dragon's tail; I've done that and got the T-shirt only to find something about making it wasn't right. Until I embarked on my own journey of self-discovery, took a good look at the guy in the mirror, and took a few punches and disappointments along the path did I figure it out: my why!

Chasing the Dragon's Tail identifies that often we fill our heads and not our hearts in our drive for happiness, self-worth, career success, well-being, and balance in our lives. I call this *"We've earned it" thinking* and we convince ourselves that is all we need to succeed. We chase the dream, the promotion, sometimes achieving our goals, only to then discover we are not happy but can't quite work out why.

The structure of this book is a journey for you, to learn about you, who you are, why you behave as you do. I will share insights for you to be your own coach and guide to achieve all you can as you find your passion and purpose.

Following this introduction, you will explore Chapter 2: Dragons Heart. This invites you to explore your values in your life and career. The information in this chapter will help you to determine your values and, most importantly, your core values which drive you. To have a Dragon's Heart is to be pure of heart. To know oneself, to embrace the universe seeking knowledge and guidance.

In Chapter 3: Dragon's Focus – Motivation, we move onto your focus; discovering what are your motivational drivers. This chapter will help you to see clearly, to have strength and focus for success with a passionate fearlessness – a dragon's focus.

Chapter 4: Dragon Whips His Tail is about starting with the end in mind by committing to your goals and aspirations and doing what you need to do to make them happen for you so you can achieve your purpose every day in every way.

Chapter 5: Dragon's Eyes – Passion. Here, you will start to determine your passions and determine more of your why. You may have heard the metaphor that your eyes are the window to your soul. The eyes of a person are said to give you insight into their inner world – their feelings and thoughts.

Chapter 6: Dragon's Wings explores the basic human need for certainty. Winged dragons in Chinese mythology are committed with certainty to getting from where they are to where they want to be. To create strategies, take risks to create certainty to achieve your aims.

Chapter 7: Dragon's Mind challenges you to examine your mindset, and determine how this may be influencing you. You will learn about the importance of your mindset in driving you, and explore ways to discover and change your mindset. Be willing for self-discovery; how to tap into your own psychic ability and intuition for answers. To the Druids, Dragons represented vitality, the psychic self, ancient wisdom, and the power of creation itself.

Be your dragon and live the dragon's life is the focus of Chapter 8: Dragon's Life. In this chapter, we explore the technique of modelling and its application to change aspects of your personal and professional life.

From your journey through this book, you will experience a renewed confidence in yourself, identify your passions, and have an insightful understanding of your purpose. You will have tools, strategies, and experiences on how to achieve fulfilment in your life. Knowing what it is to live your life on purpose, modelling in various ways from others who you admire and following your passion to find your purpose. The magic lucky number in Chinese mythology is 8. The number 8 is good fortune, wealth, and good health. Chapter 8 is therefore the luckiest number to conclude this journey to help you find passion in your purpose.

My hope with this book is that you will enjoy the journey of finding passion in your purpose and when you find it, you are able to direct it to unleash your greatest self.

Thank you - Craig Fullerton. Born in the Year of The Dragon. Chased the Dragon's Tail. Now living the Dragon Mind!

Refer to the end of this book for some special offers just for buying this book.

PART 1

VALUES AND MOTIVATION

Chapter 2
Dragon's Heart - Values

"Knowing others is intelligence; knowing yourself is true wisdom. Mastering others is strength; mastering yourself is true power." — Lao Tzu, *Tao Te Ching*

Our values inform our thoughts, words, and actions. Our values frame why we do what we do in our career, personal, and professional lives. Those that live out their values are happier being true to those values, and therefore more motivated. They receive more positive results in all they do. Values influence your motivational drivers. What drives them is based on their values, not somebody else's. NOT their boss, NOT their friends, NOT social media. They drive themselves. They are confident in themselves.

To value something means to place importance on it; anything you hold dear to you can be called a *value*. For example, if I asked you what you value most, you might answer, "Family, relationships, money, love." Let's imagine family and relationships are the *end values* that you are pursuing. As important as the other values are to you and the way you live your life, they may be considered *means values*. That is, the means to a result; a way for you to trigger the emotional states that you really desire. To further explain this, imagine I ask you, "What does family give you?" You might say, "Love, security, and happiness."

These are what you truly value and the family in this example is the means for you to achieve and live those values of love, happiness, and security. Money is a great example also. I ask you, "What does money really mean to you?" You may reply, "It gives you freedom and security." Again, like the previous example, money is merely a means to an end value. A means to achieving a much deeper set of values and emotions that you desire to experience consistently in your life.

This poses a challenge, as many people are not clear on this difference between means and ends values. Therefore, they experience a lot of frustration, emotional pain, and negative thinking and attitude in their life. Often, people are busy pursuing means values, and they don't end up achieving their true desires: their end values. Those are the values that will fulfil you and make your life rich and rewarding. I see this often around people and goal setting. They set goals without knowing what they truly value in life. Therefore, they end up either not achieving their goals as they are not associated with them at a values level, or they achieve goals at their means values and are frustrated, asking "Is that all there is?"

Values and Goals

There is an important distinction that needs to be made between values and goals. *Values* provide a deep sense of ongoing *direction* for our lives – they are not ends in themselves. *Goals* are things that we want to achieve or *do* – they are often ends in themselves. Values always exist in the *present moment*... they can be drawn on at any given moment. Goals are in the *future*.

More on the purpose of goal setting and a very efficient system that is easy to understand, quick to do, and moreover a system that you can more easily own and associate into, later.

Our values are important because they help us to grow and develop. They help us to create the future we want to experience.

Every individual and every organisation is involved in making hundreds of decisions every day. The decisions we make are a reflection of our values and beliefs, and they are always directed towards a specific purpose. That purpose is the satisfaction of our individual or collective needs.

When we use our values to make decisions, we make a deliberate choice to focus on what is important to us. When values are shared, they build internal cohesion in a group. According to the work of Richard Barrett from the Barrett Values Centre, inspired by Abraham Maslow's Hierarchy of Needs and tested with thousands of organisations, there are four types of values:

1. Individual values
2. Relationship values
3. Organisational values
4. Societal values

Personal/individual values reflect how you show up in your life and your specific needs. The principles you live by and what you consider important for your self-interest. Individual values include: *enthusiasm, creativity, humility,* and *personal fulfilment.*

Relationship values that reflect how you relate to other people in your life, whether these are your friends, family, or colleagues in your organisation. Relationship values include *openness, trust, generosity,* and *caring.*

Organisational values reflect how your organisation shows up and operates in the world. Organisational values include *financial growth, teamwork, productivity,* and *strategic alliances.*

Societal values reflect how you or your organisation relates to society. Societal values include *future generations, environmental awareness, ecology,* and *sustainability.*

For our purpose in this journey, we will be focused on personal/individual values. Values guide our every decision, and therefore, our destiny. Those who know their values and live by them become the leaders of our society. They are exemplified by outstanding individuals we witness in the world.

Values exist, whether you recognize them or not. The only way for us to be happy is to live and behave according to our true values. Otherwise we will feel internal conflict and stress. That is why it's necessary to make a conscious effort to determine your true values in life. The way we achieve this is we decide what we value most in life, and then commit to live by them every day.

Unfortunately, this attitude and action that we take in our life around our values is not common. Why is that? Maybe it's because people often don't have a clear idea of what's important to them. There are many reasons for this. In their career, for example, they may get preoccupied with ambition (e.g working towards a promotion for the sake of feeling significant or satisfying an urge to hold a senior position) that may not reflect their values. They could avoid this if only they knew what their true career values were. In their personal life, they may talk a lot about getting fit or spending more time with the family, for example, but it doesn't happen as it is very easy to talk about things a lot without tapping into your values.

Being clear on your values, making decisions, stepping up, and putting plans in place in response to your values helps to make it happen. You must be decisive in your actions around your values to achieve these aims. If you only act on them when you have time or when things become easier, for example, nothing is likely to happen. Until you are clear on your values, clear on your focus, and commit to those decisions, only then will change occur.

I am sure you have found yourself in a situation where you had a tough time making a decision about something. The most likely reason is that you weren't clear about what you value most about yourself and within the situation. Decision-making comes down to values clarification.

When you know what's most important to you, then making a decision is quite simple. Many people, though, are unclear about what's most important in their lives, so decision making becomes too hard, almost a form of internal torture manipulated by self-talk and limiting beliefs. The what-ifs and what-if-nots, the uncertainty around making a decision, the perceived external constraints, and so on are beyond restrictive. This is NOT TRUE for those who've clearly defined the highest principles in their lives.

Your values act as your personal compass to guide you through your life, your decisions towards achievement, and the success of what you want. Your values clarify the why!

Think about the most universally admired and respected people in your culture. Is it Richard Branson in the area of innovation and imagination, or is it Warren

Buffett in the area of finance? How about the late Steve Jobs in his ability to be forward thinking? Let's also look less obviously to the conductor of the local band that nurtured your training as a young musician to strive the career of your dreams as a concert artist. Maybe it was your father or mother, grandmother or grandfather. The list is endless.

Activity

Take 5 minutes right now and write a list of...
- The 5 most influential people in your life
- Why they are the most positively influential (i.e. What did they do? How did they act? What was it about them that inspired you so much?)
- Now write down how at least 3 of them have influenced why you do what you do now, how you are as a person now, and what you have chosen to do with your life now.

5 most influential people in your life:

1. ________________________________

2. ________________________________

3. ________________________________

4. ________________________________

5. ________________________________

WHY they are the 5 most influential people in your life:

1. ________________________________

2. ________________________________

3. ________________________________

4. _______________________
5. _______________________

3 of the 5: How they influenced you to be who you are today

1. _______________________
2. _______________________
3. _______________________

Reflect on those wonderful people. Notice how likely they are to have a solid grasp of their own values. Are they people who not only profess their own standards, but live by them? We all respect people who take a stand for what they believe in, even if we don't always agree with their ideas about certain things or what is their right and wrong compared to ours. There is power in individuals who commit to lead lives where their values, philosophies, and actions are one.

Most often we recognize this unique state of the human condition as a person with integrity. Culturally, there is no uniformity. These people of integrity come in many forms from many different cultural environments. The fact, however, that we cannot deny and that we observe in these people is that we perceive that their values have a tremendous influence on their culture. They have integrity, commitment, and confidence.

All of this further supports the realisation that the direction of our lives is controlled by this magnetic pull of our values. They are the force in front of us, consistently leading us to make decisions that create the direction and ultimate destination in our lives. They motivate us to move forward in all aspects of our personal and professional lives, how we make our decisions, and why we do what we do.

I have been fortunate and continue to enjoy a rich international life living and working in many parts of the world. I have been inspired by living by mountains and fjords in Norway, where people value simple living, the outdoors, and family. I have lived near the white sandy beaches in my home country of Australia. I have worked with the genuine smiles of the Filipino people, who are simply happy with what they have coupled with a strong and committed faith.

Living in China, one of the highest values in Chinese culture is that of the group rather than the individual. From thousands of years of history, an idea permanently cemented in their values is that an individual's needs must be subservient to the group's. This certainly has shaped Chinese life. As China is changing, many traditions remain, coupled with new ideas and aspects of other cultures, particularly western culture that has had varying degrees of influence on cultural values across different generations of the Chinese, and in different professional and personal contexts. There are continual shifts drifting within the values of the culture as a whole.

So, whilst there are and will always be certain foundational values one lives by, significant emotional events can create shifts in individuals. We can learn from this in our personal and professional lives as well as on a global scale that we must **get clear about what is most important in our lives and decide that we will live by those values, no matter what happens to attempt to pull us away.**

We make the decision to be consistent, regardless of whether our environment rewards us for living by our values, our standards or not. Living by our principles even when challenges appear, or we don't get the support we need and to achieve long-term happiness is to live by our highest ideals, and consistently act in accordance with what we believe our life is truly about. At times it's hard if we clearly don't know what our values are. We find it difficult, or simply cannot do this. This is the biggest tragedy.

Many people know what they want to have, but have no idea of who they want to be, or who they are. Getting things that nevertheless are achievements such as getting that new sports car, getting a promotion at work, your nameplate on your office door, going on that world holiday you've always wanted are all great things, but what if you are still not fulfilled?

In my experience as a coach, many people are not happy, but they don't know why. It is likely it's because they are not living their values. Getting things simply will not fulfil you. Only living and doing what you believe is "the right thing" will give you that sense of inner strength, confidence, and self-esteem that we all deserve.

Let's take a quiz and consider how we can find our values.

Finding Your Values

When we were children, we didn't yet understand the importance of having a clear sense of values. With our parents or other adults making our decisions based on their values, our worlds were very much influenced by the pressures that they felt in their lives.

Exercise

Close your eyes. Think back to a time and a significant event when you were 7-10 years old and you made a decision.

Take yourself back there right now. What was happening? Where were you in this event? What were you feeling? What was the day? What was the time? What was the venue of the event?

Okay, you're there...

What was the decision you had to make? No matter how minor you think it was now, back then, you were only 7-10 years old. It was a very big deal. Got it?

Now, when you made that decision, why did you make it? What were the reasons you made the decision you made?

Got it?

Could it be that, at a certain level, you were already discovering your values which led you to make a decision that you were fine with?

Isn't that interesting? There is much research that demonstrates that between the ages of 7 and 10, children start questioning. For example, they start to question if the people who hold authoritative positions, such as teachers and parents, are infallible.

Children also start to make decisions based on what

could be considered a values-understanding in such ways as developing a strong sense of what he should and should not do. For example, this often leads to the child wanting to participate in making rules for themselves and their friends, and in game play. Children of this age develop a sense of fairness and understand the necessity of rules. They understand children have rights as well and they filter rules according to what suits them.

At some level as children we were already starting to form our values. We were exploring them through decisions that we made and things we learned from our culture, our parents, and our friends, such as understanding the difference of right and wrong. However, our decisions were guided by other people's values.

To a certain extent, we develop our values as children through our trust and acceptance of some decisions made for us by others. Intuitively, we felt okay with the decision or not, based on some kind of reason, or values development. Every decision is guided by these values, even though (in most cases) as young children, we didn't set them up consciously perhaps.

Do You Know Your Values?

If I asked you to make a list of your top ten values, and write them in order of importance, could you do it? Could you decisively embrace those values with complete association, honesty, and commitment?

You may find it very difficult, or not be able to do it at all, because your mind would wander with many distractions, rationalisations, and excuses. How do you make choices that you know, in the long term, will truly reflect your values and meet your deep emotional needs? Many of these are probably not based on your true values at all, but on your various roles at work, with your family, and obligations. This is because unconsciously we often confuse our true values with other people's expectations. Many of you will create a long list of what you value, but to then refine that list to your top ten and then to your top five is challenging.

Let's be honest, it's hard to hit a target when you don't know what or where it is. Knowing your values is the critical game-changer. Anytime you have difficulty in making an important decision, it's likely that it's the result of being unclear about your values.

For example, imagine that you have to make a decision to move your family to another country in connection with a new job. You know that there is going to be some risk involved, however the position, the compensation, and location all looks better and more interesting than where you are now. What would you do? How would you respond to this? I suggest how you respond and the decision you make will depend entirely on what's important to you; the end values you are looking to achieve related to personal growth, security, stability, adventure, and comfort.

Your values come from a mixed bag of experiences, lifelong conditioning, and maybe through reward and punishment, as your parents congratulated and supported you when you did things that agreed with their values. When you clashed with their values, you were perhaps punished or ignored, as children sometimes are. Maybe your teachers encouraged you when you did things they agreed with and applied some form of discipline or consequence when you clashed, challenged, or went against their views? As an adult, this same cycle was used by your friends, employers, and work colleagues. You modelled the values of your heroes, and maybe some of your non-heroes as well.

Activity – Finding Your Values

This exercise asks you to write all your values in simple key words. For example, commitment, autonomy, faith, collaboration, and so on.

The best learning experience that you will have about yourself today is through this exercise and by doing it exactly as you are asked to below. I am asking you to do it three times for further clarification as your values may vary across different environments. Find yourself a quiet space and just focus on 'YOU', while completing this activity.

List 1 – your values in life
- Make a list. It could be 3 words. It could be 100 words. It doesn't matter; just go for it, no limits.
- Then turn that list into your top 20. Give them some clarity of thought.
- Then from that list your top 10. From your list of top 10, make it your top 5.
- It's important that you break it down this way to clarify who you are and generate a better understanding of YOU.

List 2 – the same thing regarding your CAREER
List 3 – the same thing regarding your RELATIONSHIPS

Now take these three lists of your "Top 5s" and go back and redo your life list. Has it changed?

Don't be afraid! Celebrate because this is who you are.

To summarise the importance and role of values in your personal and professional life, there are underlying *core values*. The *core values* are those which frame you and your preferred values, that at an unconscious level drive your decisions. These core values are in many ways the *"game changers"* to you.

Core Values

Our core values determine what's really important and meaningful to us and drives the direction we want to go. What inspires you? What is the flame that drives you to find your passion in your purpose?

Core values are who you are in your own deepest nature, not who you think you should be in order to fit in. They're like a compass that points us to our "true north." Often, we hear that the most common regret people express on their deathbed is: "I wish I had the courage to live a life true to myself, not the life others expected of me." Living your truth with an internal state of balance and ease is ideal.

A Painful Lesson in Identifying Core Values

Just as there are emotions we desire to experience because they enable us to experience a pleasurable state, and why we move towards them, we also have those emotions that we will do whatever we can to move away from.

As a result of one such painful situation, I left a good position in senior education leadership that I had sought after for a long time to pursue what I thought was an even greater senior education leadership position. "This is the one," I thought. "This is the position that is going to enable me to use all the skills I have to help others, to finally follow my passion and be in a position of significance. This will show all the others that I am amazing in this role," or so I thought. Six months into it I 'woke up' and discovered that it wasn't all I had hoped for and it certainly wasn't resonating with my values at all – too good to be true! I was chasing the trophy, the significance, the plaque on the office door maybe but now I was away from my family and missing being involved in and contributing to a vibrant school community. Granted, my skill set had grown and I had learnt some great and useful new skills in the new role, but wasn't happy nor motivated any more. My flame was not burning very brightly and my zest for life and my career was quickly fading away.

As I look back on that experience now, I can clearly see why I applied for the position, and accepted it, when I already had recently acquired a senior position that I had been striving towards for years that was enabling me to utilise my skills. A position that granted me much autonomy to create strategies and change to move the school forward; connecting with students and community members – ticking many of the boxes, and I was with my family; so what was the purpose? Why was I continuing to look for change for the 'ultimate post' to satisfy who I thought I was?

The answer was because I didn't have clarity on what my core values were or what motivated me. I didn't have my WHY clear enough. I thought I did, but what I was searching for was another me, a me that at that time in my life wanted to be significant, autonomous, functional, important for example. There is nothing wrong with that, of course, but I was going about this the wrong way.
I am in an environment now that enables me to do many of those things and I am happier. The difference is because I am doing those things in an environment that resonates with my values and motivational drivers.

As angry and frustrated as this situation made me, and as painful as it was financially and emotionally, it provided me with one of the most valuable lessons of my life because it gave me one of the final pieces in the puzzle. Understanding these twin forces of pain and pleasure (what I valued) has helped me not only to positively influence myself and my family, but also people around the world, with greater precision.

6 Steps to Discover Your Core Values

1. Explore

Let's start off with an exercise to help you clearly identify your *core values*. Have a pen and paper or perhaps you may choose to take notes on your computer or device.

- Can you recall a moment where you felt totally

yourself? A peak moment of life when you were in your element, when everything just felt aligned? A moment when you felt happy and fulfilled? Take some time to recall this peak moment. When you're ready, take some notes describing this peak moment in some detail.

Once you've written down a peak experience of your own then...

2. Reflect

From this peak experience, think about what values were being expressed and felt in that moment. What was important to you about that moment that made it so special? Look at your top 5 values completed in the earlier exercises to help you with this.

What were the values evident in your peak experience? Any different ones perhaps that you did not identify in the previous activities? Write them down.

3. Choose

Pick one or two values that you've identified as most important to you. Write them down.

For example, 'contribution' might be the one that is most important to you. Second might be 'caring' and so on.

4. Clarify

Now write a little bit about what your chosen value (or values) means to you. Different words mean different things to different people so it's important to define what this value means to YOU in your life. For example, to me 'contribution' essentially means that I am being kind, caring; I am helping the world to become more peaceful, happy, healthy, and in harmony. Contribution is an outward flow from my innate feelings of sharing and caring towards others and in life.

5. Name

Choose a value name that feels right to YOU. Like I said, different words can mean different things for people so it's important to define how this word is meaningful to you. For example, to me contribution is an *active* word. Therefore, I may chunk my thinking more specifically and feel that in the way I mean contribution, a better word might be *inspire*. This may be a better fit for me, so I name this value 'inspire'. What are yours? Note them down.

6. Repeat

Now that you have one or two values, repeat steps 1 to 5 until you have a set of 5 to 7 values. This will be your set of CORE VALUES. You may notice the same ones coming up again and again and that's good, as it reminds you of what your values are and in everything you do you begin to notice more, and make your decisions based on those *core values*. You may find more or more specific words to clarify your values through time and experience; further discovering who you are and why you are and why you do what you do, and how you do? Always refine to keep the list to 5 to 7 core values. This keeps you clearly focused and doesn't enable your succinct list to become longer and longer to the point where you lose clarity.

Values, in the way we speak of here, are freely chosen by YOU. Your true *core values* are not imposed on you from external sources. They come from listening to your heart and tuning in to what matters the most to YOU. In order to live a life that is true to you, you must be willing to be completely honest with yourself about what you value most in life.

Values are not rules. They don't need to become rigid or static. Values may take new forms and change and develop over time.

WHAT IS DIRECTING YOU, WHAT IS YOUR FLAME?
Moving towards what motivates you

It makes sense that you and I are constantly motivated to move forwards; to do what we need to do towards achieving a pleasurable emotional state. It's also true that we value some emotions more than others.

What are the emotional states that you value most in your life?

What are the emotions that you think will give you the most pleasure? Love, success, freedom, adventure, security or...?

We will call these *'pleasurable states.'* States that we value most moving-towards values. These are the emotional states that we will make the most effort to attain because they make us feel good.

What are some of the feelings that are most important for you to experience in your life on a consistent basis?

When I ask this question at workshops, my audiences always respond with words like: success, love, freedom, security, intimacy, adventure, power, passion, health, fun. It's likely that you probably value all of these emotions and that they are all important for you to feel in your life.

However, would it be fair to suggest that you don't necessarily value them all equally? Obviously, there are some emotional states that you will strive for rather than others. This is natural as we are likely to have what we will call a *'hierarchy of values.'* That is, each person who looks at this list will see some emotional states as being more important to them than others. This *'hierarchy of values'* controls the way you make decisions in each moment. For example, you may value comfort over passion, whilst somebody else may value freedom over security.

Activity – Emotional Drivers
As you did with values, please take some time now to dig a little deeper into what *'drives'* you. What emotions *'ignite your flame, inspire and direct you and your decisions.'*

Take a moment now and discover from this list which emotions you value most. Simply, rewrite the list in your order of importance, with 1 being the emotional state you hold as most important, and 10 being least important.

From the many suggested lists of basic emotional needs, these are the most frequently listed.

Human Emotional Needs

Fill in the blanks in your order of importance:

accepted	free	protected
accepting	fulfilled	proud
accomplished	growth	reassured
admired	happy	relaxed
alive	heard	respected
amused	helped	safe
appreciated	helpful	satisfied
approved of	in control	significant
attention	included	successful
capable	independent	supported
challenged	interested	treated fairly
clear (not confused)	inspired	understanding
competent	listened to	understood
developed	loved	useful
educated	needed	valued
empowered	noticed	
focused	open	
forgiven	optimistic	
forgiving	privacy	

1. _______________________
2. _______________________
3. _______________________
4. _______________________
5. _______________________
6. _______________________
7. _______________________
8. _______________________
9. _______________________
10. _______________________

What did you learn by doing this activity and ranking your emotional drivers from 1 to 10?

From looking at your list I could probably give you some quality feedback and learn a lot about you. For example, I would know a lot about you if your number-one value was freedom, followed by adventure and power. I would know that you are going to make different decisions than someone whose top values are security, intimacy and health. A person whose number-one value is adventure will likely make decisions differently than someone whose number-one value is security. Do you think these people would drive the same kind of car? Take the same kind of vacation? Work in the same profession? Not likely!

Remember, whatever your values are and your emotional drivers, they affect the direction of your life. We have all learned through life experience that certain emotions give us more pleasure than others. For example, some people have learned that the way to achieve and have the most pleasurable emotions in their life is to have a sense of control, so they pursue the emotions that will enable them to achieve this *'pleasurable state'* with incredible energy. It becomes the dominant focus of all their actions: It shapes many things from who they will choose to have relationships with, what they will do within those relationships and how they will live. This focus will also cause them to feel quite uncomfortable in any environment where they're not in charge.

However, let's not forget that conversely, some people do link pain to the idea of control. What they want more than anything else is a sense of freedom and adventure for example. Therefore, they make decisions completely differently. Others may achieve the same *'pleasurable state'* through a different emotion such as contribution. This value causes that person to constantly ask, "What can I give? How can I make a difference?" This will send them in a different direction from the person whose highest value is control.

When you know what your values are, what your emotional drivers are, you can more clearly understand why you consistently head in the directions you do. Also, by seeing and embracing your *'hierarchy of values"*, you can understand why you may have difficulty making decisions, or why there may be conflicts in your life. If a person's number one value is freedom, for example, and number three is intimacy, these two values are incompatible but so closely ranked in their list that they will have challenges.

I often meet people who are unaware of why they are not happy in their job. They 'don't feel right' but cannot determine why. It is often because of a values conflict that they need help in discovering for themselves. They often are not motivated in their work, and emotionally 'empty' or 'unfulfilled' but don't know why?

An Unhappy Leader

A participant in one of my workshops in education leadership was trying to discover why he did not feel happy or content in his Secondary School Principal position. The conflict, as discovered later, was one of his value of significance in successfully working towards and acquiring such a position versus regularly connecting with students of all ages across the whole school. He thought he always wanted such a senior position, perhaps as reward for his successful career; the natural next step in his career; maybe a degree of entitlement at some level that he should be in such a senior position? He had travelled around for many years enjoying a career in international schools across the world. His goal was to be a secondary school principal. He was sure that is what he wanted. He was willing to do whatever he could do or needed to do to get a senior position. He held various leadership positions, always looking for the next step into a more senior position in his journey towards his Principalship.

His family supported him in his quest for these roles, leaving the stability of friends and location to move again to his next school. Moving country to country every couple of years, when a position became available, he thought would help him get closer to achieving his goal. He thought this was all part of an 'apprenticeship' to reaching his goal. In addition to these moves he incurred great expense in many ways.

He spent a lot of money and took a lot of time away from his family, studying for various certifications and two master's degrees in education leadership, because he thought that's what he had to do. As he hadn't worked in senior leadership cultures in his schools, his assumption was that you get the qualifications, you get the training, resulting in your '*golden ticket*'; your way in and you might get the job. He finally got a position as a secondary school principal. Well done!

From our conversations, he thought that initially it was going fine, he was enjoying his job, but then, after a while, after the 'honeymoon period' was over ... "*I've got the job, yes. I've made it,*" he determined that actually he was not very happy, but he couldn't work out why. As a result of some activities we were doing and some self-discovery, he said, "I've worked it out." It was to do with his values.

He discovered that he wasn't very happy as a secondary school principal, because he "loves working with students of all ages." He likes the diversity of working across multiple ages and as a secondary school principal, he doesn't have opportunities to connect and work with students as much as he would like to. If he does create opportunities, such as coaching a sports team, for example, this is only with the older students in his secondary school division.

The result of this 'self-discovery' around the value of 'connecting', he decided to resign from his principal role and pursue positions that would involve him actively across the whole school; a school of students from kindergarten through to graduating students. He obtained a whole school leadership position and is very happy. In his new role, he has the opportunity to work with students of all ages, and connect with the whole school community, which he felt he couldn't in his Principal role. The role is not perhaps as prestigious as a senior administrator, but it resonates with his values. He consistently sought significance, believing that was the 'golden trophy'; His value he thought being 'autonomy', but when he achieved it, he felt confused.

After he made a simple change in his *hierarchy of his values,* his life was instantly changed. Shifting priorities produces power. This an example of living your values which will enhance emotional and motivational drivers towards a happier life, an example of a values /motivation connection. If you're living your values, you're motivated. When you're motivated, you're happy.

Knowing your own values helps you to get more clarity as to why you do what you do and how you can live more consistently. Consider how it may also be valuable to know the values of those you work with or someone you are in, or hope to have, a relationship with. Knowing a person's values gives you a fix on their direction and allows you to have insight into their decision making.

Knowing your own *hierarchy of values* is absolutely critical because your top values are those that are going to bring you the most happiness. Ideally you want to see and feel that you are meeting all of your values every day. If you don't you are likely to experience what seems like a constant feeling of emptiness or unhappiness. We need to realise that we must accomplish our highest values first. These are our utmost priority if we are to be happy in our personal and professional life. We need to make certain we don't settle for anything less.

Closing Thoughts

A large part of living your passions with purpose is to remember that your values – whatever they are – are the compass guiding you to your ultimate destiny. They are creating your life path by guiding you to make certain decisions and take action consistently. When we lose our direction and navigation through life, it results in frustration, disappointment, and lack of fulfillment.

We are not happy because we are not focused. We are not living our values, so we are not who we truly are. Self-talk takes over with an inner voice nagging us that "Life could be more if only somehow, something was different."

There is an unbelievable power in living your values. It is a sense of certainty that you have and what you reject in all you do: your language, your physiology, and your connectedness with others. An inner peace, a total balance, and a congruency that few people ever experience.

Chapter 3
Dragon's Focus- Motivation

"Choosing our own aims and seeking to bring them to fruition creates a sense of vitality and motivation in life. The only things that derail our efforts are fear and oppression." - Brendan Burchard

Motivation

Motivation is the force that pushes us to achieve our goals, feel more fulfilled, happier and focused to improve the overall quality of our life.

Daniel Goldman, author of several books on Emotional Intelligence, identifies four elements that make up motivation.

1. **Personal drive** to achieve the desire to improve or to meet certain standards
2. **Commitment** to personal or organizational goals
3. **Initiative**, which he defined as 'readiness to act on opportunities', and
4. **Optimism,** the ability to keep going and pursue goals in the face of setbacks

Self-motivation is the best motivation as you are empowered; it is based on your decisions and your choices. People who are self-motivated, for example tend to be more organized, have good time management skills and more self-esteem and confidence. Understanding and developing YOUR self-motivation can help you take control of many other aspects of your life.

Fundamental to self-motivation is understanding what motivates YOU to do things.

Sometimes your motivation is hidden from your consciousness, hidden deep in your unconscious mind and is in fact your own personal hidden agenda that is driving your decisions. Based on various things, stress, mood, or tasks to be completed your motivation may change from hour to hour, day to day, and continue this changing pattern throughout your life. As this happens, your needs, wants, and goals will change and evolve– sometimes not serving you well.

There are two main types of motivation: *'intrinsic'* and *'extrinsic'*.

Intrinsic motivation is self-directed, something you love and want to do.

Extrinsic motivation however is motivation that is often based on the receiving of a reward, promotion or some other external incentive. This external reward motivates you to act.

The functions of both are that intrinsic motivators motivate us to perform an action or complete a task based on our own interest, personal challenge, perceived satisfaction, or happiness. We want to! Extrinsic, on the other hand, are motivators based on obtaining some sort of external prize, reward, or promotion for example. In school it may be to get good grades; in business it may be to attain power or promotion or more money, for example. A motivator coming from outside – not intrinsic or internal.

Different people are motivated by different things and at different times in their lives. Sometimes the same task may have more intrinsic motivators and more extrinsic motivators at other times. Most tasks will have a **combination of the two types** of motivation.

I'm sure you can appreciate that we all tend to work better when we love what we are doing. If we are inspired and happy with our job, it's easier to get out of bed each morning to go to work. When thinking about what motivates you to perform a certain task or embrace certain things, think about both intrinsic and extrinsic motivators. Those days when you struggle to get motivated, write down the motivators and see if they are from within or external. This may help you determine why you feel that way.

Motivation Is a Key to Success

We all aim for success in life, but getting there is a journey, not a race. Motivation is the fuel that will keep you moving towards the top of your mountain; to achieve your journey. Motivation is a trickster – hard to grasp and then often hard to keep.

Motivation is fed by two things:
- The *desire* to *attain* something
- The *fear* of *losing* something

To achieve success, desire is the key to staying motivated. When we act out of fear, we are in a reactive state. When we act out of desire, we can stay focused and follow a constructive path.

How do we keep desire from fading? There are many ways to keep the fire and drive alive. It's often suggested that we become like the people with which we spend the most time with. Therefore, surrounding yourself around positive, motivating people will push you to do better and work towards reaching your goal. Seeing other people who are self-motivating will also encourage you and teach you how to motivate yourself and fuel that desire to attain your goals.

Negative communication – whether it's in your own mind or with and around others only fuels negative behavior and can hold you back. Communicating in a positive way will help you stay motivated, and help you motivate others. Smile and live positively, say positive things.

Try it today with people you work with, or your family members, or at your next meeting.

Try it and you will also feel positive and stay in a positive state throughout the day. It's not hard to do!

Your mood is affected by two different things: your physiology and your energy. What does it mean to say that your mood is determined by your physiology? Consider the signs and energy that a motivated person radiates. They smile, laugh, and they more often than not shine with consistent optimism. They often have better posture and more approachable body language than someone who's not as motivated. It's true that certain goals and experiences cause these reactions. Conversely, being happy, open to change, and optimistic also work the other way, making you susceptible to positively evaluating the task at hand, your life, and what the future brings if you accomplish your objectives. This can help you get motivated and discover what **drives you**.

A quote that continues to resonate with me is *"The fact is that we live only on such a small percentage of our potential: you do not allow yourself to be totally yourself, society does not allow you to be totally yourself."* Bruce Lee

I was only 14

As a 14-year-old, my sporting involvement to date had been in swimming, which I enjoyed and was quite good at. Each afternoon, I would travel to the pool to train with the local swimming club. I trained hard and whilst not a 'natural sportsman' and average at the other strokes, I discovered that my 'claim to fame' was what some consider the hardest stroke in the pool – the butterfly. I did well to competitively achieve some great results for my age group. A 'tick' there for self-esteem and to be amongst the cool kids at that age. More interesting was that I discovered I was a person that wanted to explore different things than my friends. Believe me not many of my friends were at all interested in the butterfly.

For me the motivation to swim was purposeful for two main reasons. I wanted to be fitter and lose weight, I was certainly not as 'lean' as some of my friends – let's leave it at that for now, but I wasn't particularly interested in team sports. I preferred to give myself my own goals and was determined to achieve them. I was also a musician which for a 14 year old in middle school at that time was certainly not cool according to many of the 'lads' who decided that I was an easy target to bully – so my journey through the early years of secondary school consisted of a lot of bullying, physical and mental. What was I doing wrong was my self-talk for those few years, why me? As you can understand life at school was not as much fun for me as it could have been. My musician mates were older than me so we would spend a lot of the break time in the music room have a great time making music, playing in school productions and so on. After school I would try and forget the negative parts of the day by training hard in the pool and rehearsing with the local band for a couple of evenings each week.

Inevitably with my inquiring mind as to what I truly could be capable of – a trait that has remained with me throughout my life journey and wanting to learn what our mind's amazing potential is- I was self-motivated to embark on a mission for self-improvement, to be cooler, fitter, to fit in better with my own age group – or more importantly to be more self-confident with the choices I had made and to stand up for myself to these bullies. I embraced this motivation with enthusiasm, excitement, and a raw energy to do all I could to facilitate this change I wanted for myself. I chose to begin my martial arts journey. At that time in the small town where I lived, this was probably the most non-typical sport for a kid my age, let alone me, who was already cast aside by some for being a musician as well.

To put this in context, growing up in a small country town in Australia in the 1970's and 1980's, there were social norms one would expect to adhere to as a boy if one was to be accepted amongst his peers. When it came to hobbies and sport those norms were, you play in the local football team, maybe tennis and that's about it. Right from the 'get go', I was way out of sync – playing music at school and on weekends with the local brass band, then putting swimming and learning martial arts with that – I have a recipe for personal teenager disaster!

I laugh now as The Way of Martial Arts, the self-discovery aspects and mindset tools, besides the physical skills that I was learning quickly became a passion and have mapped much of why my values are what they are, why I am writing this book for you right now – from a passion to share tools and educate as many people as I can to become who they truly are, and do what they passionately want to do – to find what motivates them, embrace it and allow these motivators to drive them to success and happiness.

It all started with motivation and living that motivation with commitment to achieve success. Who was to know at 14 simply by embracing every aspect of a simple motivation "I want to be fitter and be more confident," it would change my life and underpin who I am, my musical and professional journey; my journey on discovering and learning as much as I could about the potential of the human mind.

Interestingly, now all these years later I find myself at the heart of martial arts thinking, living and working in China and still training, still learning all I can about martial arts, its spirituality, its history and its application to 'real life'. I might be a bit slower on skills than I was at 14 but I am still very much a 'martial artist' in my approach to living and loving life.

"It is not how much you have learned, but how much you have absorbed in what you have learned." - Bruce Lee

What is Motivation?

"Purpose provides activation energy for living." - M. Csikszentmihalyi, 'Flow'

Focusing on motivation towards your success, towards what you want rather than motivation away from what you don't want is the key.

The areas of knowledge and evolution of what we know surrounding things such as philosophy, psychology and neuroscience share a common theme of unlocking human potential. They do this by leveraging reason and the full power of the mind. "I *think* therefore I *am* and I *do*." Motivated people embrace this truth. Great artists, leaders, and innovators are so because they utilize their entire values, belief systems, and power of their reasoning to do what they need to do to become their highest selves, and do their highest good.

They know who they are and express it openly and pursue meaningful goals towards success. They are often Masters of strategy who carefully contemplate their direction; they determine what will give them the greatest sense of fulfillment and energy in every major decision they make. Often 'labelled' as the 'lucky ones', they are just like you and I. They decided to *choose* wisely. People who are motivated are not 'lucky', they are simply conscientious, choosing to use their minds on purpose to energize and enrich their lives. Taking this approach, they tend to achieve more and therefore gain more respect.

The person who is in charge of their own mind and emotions, has extraordinary power and earns high regard.

The person not in charge of their own mind is lost in a 'soup' of unpredictable and often unwanted thoughts and impulses, often being overcome by fear, self-doubt and social despair. I think we realize that motivation is not an accident, it is a feeling, a more conscious commitment; a deeply felt principle to take action; an energy that results from thinking on purpose. We feel motivated because we choose to, not because we hope to get lucky.

If we want more motivation in our lives, we must make clearer choices and more deeply commit to them.

With self-motivation, focus, and decision, there is freedom which helps you to achieve your success. Freedom pulls so strongly at your heart because of the human desire for ascension. That is, our natural drive to rise from our circumstances and actualize our goals, our potential, our highest self. Seeking to soar in life takes determination, struggle and courage. Freedom involves us engaging with our 'true self' and our ambitions, leading to independence, growth and happiness. Those who make the effort achieve their goals and vision.

Through the pursuit of personal freedom, you will discover your destiny; through fear may result in your demise. You can feel motivated to either move forward or to halt, to grow or not, to settle or to strive for change and greatness. If you lack compelling reasons to take action then you will tend to stay put, and always hope for greatness but never achieve it. If you have a strong list of reasons to move forward you are more likely to consistently advance your life.

Success and fulfillment in life rests on the unflagging

ability to follow your passions on purpose, to be true to yourself, to chase your dreams and visions with fire each day, More broadly, our entire human value system rests on motivation. None of the great human values that keep us and society in check such as kindness, love, honesty, fairness, unity, tolerance, respect, and responsibility would flourish if we were not motivated to bring them to life. This means if we fail to master our motivation as individuals, we are not likely to be happy.

Imagine how the world could change if people were able to tap into their motivation whenever desired, for as long as desired. Imagine yourself being motivated more of the time how much happier and free you would be. True motivation is embedded deep within you and is the driver of your success and focus. When you find it, know it, embrace it, and live it.

Finding your Motivation

Finding your motivation is not a difficult thing to do and can be a self-inspiring process. To begin you need to determine WHY you do what you do? Motivation has its core a 'reason for action'. It's the 'why' you do something. To develop a motive for action, your mind with or without conscious guidance, filters through various thoughts, feelings, and experiences, and *chooses* from them a set of reasons to do or not to do something. Your mind's clarity on and commitment to your choices determines your level of motivation. If you are clear and committed, you will feel a high level of motivation. If you are unclear or uncommitted, motivation will be low.

The driver of motivation is choice

Your mind chooses a reason for action. It either committed to that choice or it didn't. Therefore, you experience a high level of motivation or a low one. This is how you find your greatest 'personal power'. Personal Power is your ability to control your impulses and direct your minds to choices and commitments that will serve you; your goals and aspirations. You can choose your aim, and your reasons for that aim, with continual focus on achieving your aims and goals. This will create a desire to take action, to make it happen. This you will sense as energy from within - a strong intrinsic motivating driver, a motivating power that if strong enough will keep you focused on where you want to be and what you want to achieve. A hallmark of those who achieve greatness is the discovery that they can control the level of motivation they feel by better *directing their own minds on purpose from within.*

Motivation creates its spark from the energy you create. This energy is created by being clear on your goals, ambitions, and expectations. Your ambitions based on your goals are the *choices you have* to be, to have, to do, or to experience something greater than you are experiencing now in your life. Your motivation is your energy. You keep that energy high. The stronger your desire, the higher the sense of motivation you will feel.

Activity

To start to clarify your intrinsic motivational drivers, ask yourself the following:

- What do I want for myself?
- What new goal would be meaningful to me?
- What am I excited about learning or giving to others?
- What incredible new adventure do you dream of?
- What can I pursue or who can I serve above myself that will give me the energy to look forward to each day?

Write down your responses to start feeding your ambitions and therefore your motivations. If you deeply contemplate and affirm higher aims, you energize yourself to pursue them.

You see, read, and hear every day that many people, including ourselves, want something better. They have exciting and enthusiastic ambitions, but they still are not motivated. Why? Because they don't *believe it can happen* for them, or they can't *make it happen*, they feel in a state of 'lack'. That is, they expect it *not to happen*.

Consider a budding entrepreneur who wants to start a business and go out on his own but doesn't leave the security of his existing job as he has convinced himself that he cannot make it on his own – "It won't happen, I can't do it, too hard" is his daily mantra, his daily self-talk. So, guess what - "perception is projection" - he gets what he expects. He doesn't pursue his dream and is content to stay unhappy yet secure in his current job. He has the desire without the belief to succeed, so he won't even try. The 'game-changer' here is that his expectancy to not succeed is the difference between just hope and actual motivation.

Simply by changing your mindset you can move

towards having the motivation and achieving your goals. Trust yourself to know that you will have success. Have faith and belief in yourself to achieve your goals. You have the WHY, you have the WHAT. Step up and make it happen and then the HOW will appear once you have embraced and committed to your goals, you are self-motivated and focused. For example, instead of saying to yourself "what if; but; too difficult," create an affirmation like this, that, if repeated and embraced every day you will start to see the change and the results you want.

Affirmation: *"I expect that 'it' (whatever your it is) will happen no matter what, because I have faith and believe in myself to learn and grow every day. I am focused and energized towards (my goal) and know and trust that I know what I need to and will do every day to make it happen"*

With these committed and constant expectations, your mind begins to form behaviors needed to make your ambitions a reality.

Dream a Little Dream
Take some paper and a pen and spend some time today to *focus* your mind and see, imagine, associate into, and feel your dreams coming true, see yourself making it happen for you.

- Find a comfortable place to sit, no distractions, and just relax and spend some time with your thoughts. Think about what would bring happiness and fulfillment into your life if you could have it NOW?

- Write it down, imagine it. Be specific what would it look like, feel like. Where would it be, what would you be doing, how would it change your life, how would it drive you to be motivated to make it happen?
- NOW look at what you wrote down and refine it, make it more specific, how would it motivate you? Coach yourself - what you would need to do to constantly have that motivation to achieve it, to succeed.
- Make your wording focused on purpose. You are committed intrinsically to being motivated towards this and that you will do what you need to do to maintain a strong and committed motivation.

Reflect: Consider the person who wants to compete in a triathlon. In order to succeed she knows that she cannot tell herself over and over again, as she has done already for many years that "I hope one day I get good enough to maybe do a triathlon." If she does what will happen - yes, you got it, she will always be "hoping to do a triathlon one day". Instead she summons up her motivation and makes the choice to begin to train, to succeed, because she believes she *must* and believes she *can*.

Read out loud, turn up the music.

- There is no specific commitment to that. Instead she flips her mindset and clarifies WHY she has this ambition, and tells herself that she will race to the best of her ability and succeed.

- She visualizes herself in the water flying through the swim leg, exiting the water so fast she almost forgets her cycle shoes as she runs towards her bike, picks it up, gets on the seat and rides like the wind, feeling the breeze in her hair, the water from the swim keeping her body cool as she moves her legs as fast as she can.
- Completing the bike leg, she runs and runs like her life depends on it; a big smile on her face, knowing she has completed her race; her dream to do a triathlon.
- She crosses the finish line, throws her arms up in a euphoric feeling of achievement, happiness - all because she changed her thinking, to motivation and commitment to do this.

So, to those that say "I wish I were more motivated", we respond with "Do not hope for motivation; choose ambition and goals to become motivated for." Focus on that dream and believe it will happen. You will soon find a great stream of energy and enthusiasm will enliven you. Therefore, the sustaining choices of motivation are *attention and effort. Focus and action. Commitment and Belief in yourself. YOU be* the *Game-Changer.*

By giving your goals and ambitions consistent focus and attention will keep the drive alive; your energies always swirling and moving in anticipation of success. Journaling, visualizing, and thinking about them are simple consistent ways to keep this focus on fulfillment and achievement of those ambitions.

"We mustn't let our dreams die in the daylight because we lose focus while responding to other interests or false emergencies that the world will present us"

– Craig Fullerton

The win-win secret is the deeper and longer you give attention to your ambitions and passions, the more motivation you will feel. There is a *value-motivation connection.* If you are living your values, you're likely to be more motivated. When you're motivated, you're likely to be happier and more fulfilled.

Not everyone is born with motivation. There is a severe lack in some who believe 'I'll get to that one day' or 'the timing isn't right' or a classic case of 'I can't do that'. Motivation is the defining factor that turns a good thought into immediate action. It turns a good idea into a business and can positively impact the world around you.

Without motivation, you can't achieve anything. There are no goal posts to aim for and no purpose to strive towards.

Motivation is an **important life skill**. The reason it's important is because every person on this earth is unique and has a purpose. To implement and monitor your purpose well, you have to be motivated to work towards your goals which helps your dreams become a reality. Not just for your sake, but the sake of others as well.

For example, if Steve Jobs wasn't motivated to start Apple, you wouldn't have a MacBook Air, iPhone, or iPad.

You wouldn't be wearing that designer watch if a designer wasn't motivated to turn their visualization into a realization.

You live in a world where motivation has solved

problems and produced products and services you never knew you needed.

Motivation can also help you personally to be the best you can be. This can have a positive effect on your confidence, self-esteem, relationships, and the community you live in.

If you're still not convinced about building up your motivation, here are eight reasons why motivation is important in life.

1.   Motivation Clarifies A Goal

When you're motivated, you embrace a desire to change your life. Motivation pushes you towards your goal because of a desire for change. Motivation helps you clarify your goal so you know exactly what you're working towards.

2.   Motivation Sets Priorities In Life

Once you know what your goals are, motivation helps you prioritise your life. If your goal is to write a book, you need to set time aside each week to write it. Motivation helps you to focus and make a commitment to seeing your goal accomplished.

3.   Motivation Pushes Through Setbacks

Every road to success is likely to have a setback. There is no such thing as a dream route to reach your dreams. Setbacks will have you doubt whether your goal is worth the effort, but *motivation steps in* and gives you the strength and courage to try again.

4.   Motivation Teaches Perseverance

This ties in with the previous point, but motivation helps you strive through setbacks, trials and fears. Thomas Edison is known for the invention of the light bulb and is noted for this quote, *"I have not failed. I've just found 10,000 ways that won't work."* He also inspired this thought, *"Our greatest weakness lies in giving up. The most certain way to succeed is always to try just one more time."* Motivation will teach you to persevere when reality and your internal self-talk tells you to give up.

5.   Motivation Fights Against Fear

Fear of failure is so common it can literally stop you from taking action. Motivation kicks fear in the butt because it tells it, *no matter what I'm feeling, I'm going to do it anyway.* Motivated people see beyond their fear and can visualize the outcome. Motivation will always help you see the bigger picture.

6.   Motivation Builds Self-Confidence

When you're motivated to achieve your goal, confidence is a result of the small steps taken to see that goal achieved. When you've pushed through setbacks and fear, there is a sense of accomplishment and this builds an inner confidence to try something new. Motivated people will have a few projects on the go because they have pushed through barriers and seen positive results, which gives them motivation to start new projects and try new things.

7.   Motivation Attracts Your Mentor

If you've ever met a motivated person, they have an energy, a vibe that is alluring and inspiring. You feel attracted towards who they are because you want to align with their energy, so you can draw from their expertise. In turn, this helps build your motivation to succeed.

The same can be said of a business manager. If you require a team to help you achieve your dream, a good leader will know how to use their motivation to pioneer a spirit of drive and desire within the team to see results. Employees will want to work *with you and for you* if they are valued and can take hold of the vision by their leader.

8.   Motivation Inspires Others

Motivation is an attractive trait and it can inspire others to make things happen in their own life. If you've ever met or spent time around self-motivated people, you instantly feel like you can achieve anything because their positivity and can-do attitude elevates your own spirit. Seeking out motivated people can help elevate your own motivation levels.

Take away: Motivation is a muscle that needs to be constantly worked and this can be achieved by reading biographies, enrolling in training and listening to motivational speakers who can share their own successes, while building you up. Listen and read about these people; choose a mentor from them who you can follow their journey and model in your own life aspirations and goals.

Chapter 4
Dragon Whips His Tail -Start With the End in Mind

Motivation and Goals

"A purpose is the eternal condition of success." - Bruce Lee

No excuses! If you want to achieve greatness, you need to stop asking for permission. This is why motivation is important in life because it stops asking questions and aligns you to work towards your goals. Commit to being, doing, and having.

Goals are the stepping stones towards your dreams, so in order to achieve them, you need motivation to keep you moving towards them.

The Basic Tool For Greatness And Motivation is Goal Setting

"The future does not get better by hope, it gets better by plan. And to plan for the future we need goals." – Jim Rohn

Do you set goals for yourself? If you wrote them down – NOW – what would be your goals for the next year, the next 3 years, the next 5 years or 10 years? What are your aspirations for your life?

Consider these:

"The trouble with not having a goal is that you can spend your life running up and down the field and never score."
– Bill Copeland

"You need to plan to build a house; to build a life, it is even more important to have a plan or goal." – Zig Ziglar

Goal setting is the first step of successful goal achievement. It marks your first point towards success. It is when you are decisive and choose to move from a passive state to being involved in taking control of your life.

7 Important Reasons Why You Should Set Goals

1. To Stop Plodding Through Life
Many people today are plodding through life, simply existing. Even though they work hard, they don't feel like they are getting what they want. That's because they don't have a direction of where they want to go, what they want to achieve. For example, students graduate and they're not sure what to do with their life; adults work for years and are shocked when they reach their 30s/40s and they don't know what to do next, or they find that they have not really been happy; their job hasn't reflected their values or resonated with their motivation in a long time. They realise that they have not been fulfilled, they have simply been working a J.O.B- and are 'Just **Over Broke**', living hand to mouth for example only to cover their bills and living expenses – working to live.

As Bill Copeland says, when you don't set goals, you can spend your whole life running up and down and not achieve anything. In reality you're just fulfilling others' goals; your bosses, your colleagues, your friends, your relationships, but not yours. It can be the fast food industry telling you to eat fast food because you're "lovin' it." It can be the consumer goods industry telling you that you need this shampoo with 79% frizz-reduction formula because it'll make your life better. It can be fashion labels getting you to buy their clothes because you supposedly look cooler in them. It can be many things outside of you.

When you stop to set goals and think about what you want, you break out of autopilot and start living a life of your conscious creation. Instead of letting others tell you what to do, you proactively take charge and think about what you want for yourself.

2. To Get Maximum Results

Top performers, world-class athletes, and successful people set goals. Michael Phelps (competitive swimmer and most decorated Olympian of all time), Mark Zuckerberg (co-founder of Facebook), Richard Branson (creative entrepreneur) , and Elon Musk (CEO of SpaceX and Tesla Motors) all set goals. That's because when you set goals, you have a vision to work towards. You ensure that you are pushing yourself to get the best results, rather than resting on your laurels and waiting for things to happen. You need to take action or your goals will not happen.

Know that what gets measured gets improved. If you don't set specific targets and goal-posts along your journey and celebrate achievements and milestones, how are things going to improve? There is literally nothing to work towards, and even though you may be working hard, your hard work may not translate into anything. As the popular saying goes, *"Shoot for the moon. Even if you miss, you'll land among the stars."* When you set goals, you are aiming for the moon. Your goals propel you to take more action than you would have otherwise.

Ask yourself: What do you want to see for yourself 1 year from now? How about 3 years from now? 5 years? When you set goals, you think ahead, after which you can create your action plan. Even if things don't go according to plan, that's okay as you can review, adjust your plans, and then steer your life towards your vision; keep focused towards achieving your goals and living your vision.

Know that all things are created twice: first in the mind, then in the physical world. The mental creation happens when you set your goals. The physical creation happens when you work on your goal and bring it to life. Without the mental creation, the physical creation can't happen. When you set goals, you kick off the very first step to make your dreams happen, after which the next steps will follow suit.

3. To Create Laser-Like Focus

Goals give you focus. While a life purpose gives you the general direction, your goals give you laser focus as to what exactly to spend your time and energy on.

For example, let's imagine you set a goal to create a small business, like a café. Even though you have no idea how to make it happen, the very act of setting a goal gives you a focal point. As you brainstorm for ideas, you realize that you can start by studying the local environment, the coffee shops, the cafes. See what they are doing; do a comparative study; look at how you can create your uniqueness, so people will come to you for their coffee and snack, rather than the other shops. Understanding what people are looking for in that environment, what do they like. What could you introduce to be different than the competition, what services could you provide in your coffee shop that people would want to come back every day and bring their friends? Then, take barista and baking classes to master your skills. At the same time, test recipes and let your friends taste your creations before selling them.

Think of your energy as the input and the results as the output. When you have a goal, you create a focal point where your energy can be channeled to create maximum reward. Be specific with your goal, otherwise you have no goal. For example, your goal might be to initially achieve 1000 visitors a week, and have that grow to 5000. Putting the figures out there will further help you to prioritize and identify the most important tasks you need to do to achieve this traffic target, while eliminating low-value tasks that do not contribute to this vision.

Students, as a comparison, can transfer this mindset to create a goal to achieve A's, for example. How? You prioritize and identify the key action steps to achieve the best grades. Strategies you commit to achieve this might be doing all you can, mixing with the 'right' people to assist you in selecting the best class combination for optimal grades, studying past exam papers, consulting your teachers, finding a mentor, and having a study timetable, while eliminating time wasting tasks like excessive use of social media and binge-watching TV shows. This then creates maximum results.

4. To Create Accountability

Having goals makes you accountable. Rather than just talk, you are now obligated to act. This accountability is to yourself, not anyone else. No one knows the goals you set. Other people also don't stand to gain anything from you achieving your goals. The focus is you and your commitment, doing what you can towards your achievements. By setting specific targets, you can easily see if you are on track, and if not, what to do about it.

When I started writing articles and speaking. I set goals, for example to complete and post a certain number of articles a week, to create a regular presence and hit a certain traffic target each week, to create a certain number of speaking opportunities each quarter and to get a certain number of coaching clients per month. This made me accountable to these targets. Each week, I would monitor my performance while working on my plan. If I found myself falling short, I would take the necessary steps to address it. I would cut out my 'time wasting tasks' and identify the actions needed to achieve my goals. Doing so helped me grow my online presence, coupled with creating a regular following from my speaking engagements, moving closer to my personal plan within a year to turn my passion into my full-time career.

5. To Motivate Yourself

When you set goals, you connect yourself with your innermost desires. They help motivate yourself and give you something to strive for. This is especially powerful if you're not in a good place in life at any moment. Your goals help remind you of the things you love, to redirect your focus away from the negative obstacles, and to reconnect you with your innermost desires.

Henry Ford once said, *"Obstacles are those frightful things you see when you take your eyes off your goal."* When you are feeling negative and down, it's often because you feel you've nothing worth looking forward to.

Your goals are the calmness to strive for, to push you out of the storm.

If I ever lost motivation, I would reflect, relax, and focus on some of the most important goals in my life. I would visualize the scenario with full clarity, as if it is happening now. This connects me with my inner self right away as I remember my WHY. This is your deepest motivation, after which I'd feel energized and get to work right away.

6. To Always Be The Best You Can Be

Goals help you achieve your highest potential. Without goals, you default to a routine of activities that keeps you feeling safe and comfortable each day. But this familiarity restricts any growth. It denies you from tapping into your infinite potential.

By setting goals, you set targets to strive towards. These targets make you venture into new places and new situations that put you into growth mode. For example, setting a time limit for your morning workout lets you know if you should be working out more efficiently in the time you have given yourself. Setting a weight loss target helps you know if your actions have been effective in losing weight. Setting a career goal ensures that you are not settling for anything less than what you desire.

7. Strive to Live Your Best Life

Last but not least, goals ensure that you get the best out of life.

Whether you want this or not, time will pass in your life. In one year, you'll be one year older. In five years, you'll be five years older. Goals with specific measures and deadlines ensure that you are maximizing your experience in your world. If you already feel you have discovered your life purpose, your goals will help you get the best out of your purpose.

Imagine this: The world is your oyster. There are millions, billions of things you can do, experiences you can have, and people you can encounter. There are endless possibilities of what you can accomplish. What if you can do whatever you want? What do you want to achieve? What do you want to see, do, and experience in your life? Set your goals, make them happen, and watch as you create your best life ever.

Start Setting Goals

To get started ask yourself this: **What are my goals for the upcoming 1 year, 3 years, 5 years, or even 10 years?**

If you just take some time out to follow the process explained below and set your goals now, I can guarantee you that you will definitely experience more growth. By just spending a few minutes to articulate some aspirations that have been in your mind, you will experience more progress in your life a year from now than if you don't.

Time to have some fun and make some noise!

Step 1: Setting clear, concise goals creates Your Map to Success

The first step to produce results in your life is to get very clear on what you want to achieve. You need to begin to take control of your goals by thinking carefully about what goals you have set and why you have set them. Without determining the 'why', your goals are simply words on a page that mean nothing, or at the most just an idea.

- You must *do* your goals!
- *Own* your goals!
- Be *Empowered!* Be Passionate on Purpose.
- Be *in charge*! and Always know the *why*.

The more specific you define your outcome focus, the better your chances are of attaining it.

1. Think about the *why*.
2. Gain clarity on it. Be specific.
3. Commit to your goals absolutely – What would it mean for you if you embraced these 100%?
4. Navigate your future. Imagine how much you will achieve by knowing what you want, why you want it, and how you're going to achieve it.

Consider this:

1. Where would you rather be?
2. Where are you now and where do you want to be in the future?
    - Next month?
    - Next week?
    - Next year?
    - In five years?

What about if you had incredibly powerful tools and techniques to get you there as quickly as possible?

Read on ...

"I believe we are meant to celebrate the past and live fully in the now while consciously creating the future."
- Christopher Howard

Take a deep breath, get excited, and let the journey begin.

Create Your Life Vision
Firstly take a few minutes to think about what you want your life vision to look like. This will be based on what you are committed to achieving in your life. How you want to live your ideal life. Then note your WHY. It starts with your why – to get clarity on your goals. WHAT your life vision will look like is because of your ownership and clarity on the WHY.

Note it in the spaces below. It doesn't have to be perfect. It just needs to give you a sense of direction towards achieving what you want and deserve, and why you want it.

- *WHAT* I really want to achieve in my life and *WHY* I want it.

My Vision Is:

____

____

____

____

____

____

____

____

____

____

____

____

____

____

Now 'chunk' your thinking down to specifically identify specific goals to get you to where you want to go; to help you attain your vision. Think about specific goals and note each of them down in detail to start with.

- What I really want to **achieve in** (insert your goal).

My goal is to have/be/do:

____

Now:

____

____

____

____

____

____

____

____

____

Next Month:

____

____

____

____

____

____

____

Three months:

____

____

____

____

____

____

____

____

____

____

____

A year:

____

____

Five years:

Ten years:

> How do you feel now? Taking the time to think about these goals. You will find writing them down is empowering. Every word you write is empowering you, motivating you, and associating you towards achieving your goal.

You have taken the first step to achieving your goals and being in control of your future! *Your* goals and *your* vision may change over time, and that's ok. Don't worry about trying to get them absolutely perfect straight away. Review them regularly and re-write them as you feel the need to. This will happen as you find yourself getting clearer about what you want. Now that you have defined your *future vision* you are focused on where you want to be and the results you want to achieve.

Step 2: Break down your Life Vision by setting your specific goals.

Setting of your specific goals will act as markers on your journey and checkpoints for your success. These markers will guide you towards your vision and keep you on track.

Each time you surpass each goal, celebrate the achievement, and be reminded you are keeping your focus and increasing your confidence with each success.

When setting goals for any area of your life, remind yourself of the most important questions over and over –

- WHAT DO YOU WANT?
- WHY DO YOU WANT IT?

The HOW will take care of itself later, you will know at the right time when the how is revealed to you. Many people are their worst enemy and never achieve their dreams because they become too concerned about how they could possibly get from point A to point B. It all seems too hard so it never happens. They never achieve their goals for FEAR of not achieving them!

Take Alice for example.

'Would you tell me please, which way I ought to go from here?' 'That depends a good deal on where you want to go,' said the Cat. 'I don't much care where,' said Alice. 'Then it doesn't matter where you go,' said the Cat." – Lewis Carroll.

Without knowing where you're going, you will end up like Alice in Wonderland, feeling lost, wandering around without direction or purpose, depending on others to tell you where to go.

How true these words are. Without focus and association of where you want to go, why you want to go there, how will not appear, so you won't find and celebrate your true potential?

C.R.E.A.T.E Your Future

It is paramount that you word your goals precisely,

realistically, <u>towards what you want</u> *(not away from what you don't want)* and that you can clearly see, feel, and associate into what is the end result. <u>The end result is the key</u>. If you can see the result focus, associate into that end step, it becomes 'real' and therefore is more likely to actually happen.

<u>C.R.E.A.T.E Criteria:</u>
C - Clear and concise.
R - Realistic.
E - Ecological – safe to you and safe to others.
A - Act as if 'now'.
T - Timed and towards what you want.
E - End step, evidence that you achieved your goal.

C - Clear and concise

It is important that each of your goals be expressed as specific and concise. Being specific brings what are just ideal goals written on a page into reality. Being concise with your wording, you create a 'succinct statement'. A concise 'nutshell' statement makes it all the easier to focus on achieving the goal, both with your conscious and unconscious mind. A clear and concise goal can be more easily actualized, rather than a goal that is worded without giving clear instructions to your unconscious and conscious mind. Clear instructions equals clear focus. With a clear and concise goal focus, the resulting energy generated from this will be more committed towards you achieving your goal.

R – Realistic

It is important when writing your goals to set ones that

you expect you can achieve. Realistic means what is achievable to you. You can set your goals as big or as small as you like. Consider, that if you have never achieved what you want in life then scale your goals back by making them more attainable. Conversely if you have always achieved what you want, make your goals bigger – stretch your thinking! As the saying goes, *nothing breeds success like success,* so it is important that you write goals in a way that you honestly believe resonates with you and you will achieve them. When you reach your goals, you will experience an incredible feeling of power and success. This empowerment will continue to feed more and more success as you become more and more confident that you can achieve all you expect to and more. **Remember, you get what you expect, what you decide!**

E- Ecological and ethical to you, others, and the environment

Think about what the consequences are likely to be when you achieve your goal? Is the outcome going to be safe for you and for others? If you decide YES, then you know it is probably a good goal to set – a Win-Win!

A – Act as if 'now'

You must write your goals in **present tense**. That is because once your mind has imagined something is happening now – in the present, it is far easier to accomplish. If something is happening now, you can imagine associating into it right now! The unconscious mind doesn't know the difference between what is imagined and what is real. It has no concept of time – it's unconscious!

The unconscious mind is our lifeline- it pumps our blood around our body; it operates our digestive system; it beats our heart; produces cells; gives us a new stomach lining every 7 days; it blinks our eyelids – it is our lifeline; it runs our supercomputer – the brain. It doesn't know the difference between what is vividly imagined and what is real. To visualize a goal as if it were happening right now, it becomes more achievable and compelling. So, write your goal in the present tense language, as if you are living it in that very moment you write it down, right now!

T – Timed and towards what you want
When writing your goals in present tense, you need to allocate a future date or time when you will reach the goal. This specific information clearly indicates when you wish to achieve the outcome. Without committing your goal to a particular date and time, it will always be a 'want' and only exist vaguely sometime in the future, so it might never actually happen. For example, I am sure you are familiar with ***"Success is right around the corner."*** If you say that to yourself ten times a day, surely you will achieve success. Probably not because this is not a clear, concise, specific, or a 'as now' goal focus. Let me explain.

These questions are not addressed specifically in the wording of this as a goal.
- *When will you be successful? What day and date, specifically?*
- *Around what corner?*
- *Where will you be successful?*
- *What do you mean by success, specifically?*

Can you see now what I mean?

A better-worded goal would be:

It is (date)

____

And, I am

____ **(as now)**

For example:
 It is now _27 July 2020 and I am looking at my_ **graduation certificate that shows that I received distinctions for all my subjects.**

*This is specifically worded and timed towards what you want.

A goal is a dream with a deadline!

The 'T' as mentioned also means your goal should be 'towards' what you want. It is important to express your goal positively – _towards what you do want_, rather than any negative language that suggests your goal is focused _away from what you don't want._
　　For example, your focus in your wording of your goal would **not** be "I am no longer fat." Rather you would write, "I weigh _______(insert my ultimate weight)_ and I feel awesome."

Your focus determines your results in life. Your words must direct your focus towards what you do want, not away from what you don't want!

E – End Step

This step, this end result empowers you and makes it real, makes your goal achievable. Always include this final step as your evidence, your proof that you have achieved your goal. In the example above, the end step was that you were looking at your graduation certificate that showed you had achieved all distinctions, on July 27 2020. This is specific.

Alternatively, if your goal was "I have passed my exams and graduated." As encouraging as that sounds, to make it happen it needed to follow the CREATE criteria to **make it real at an unconscious as well as conscious level**.

This end step, this evidence, is your ultimate visualization, your proof that you have reached and achieved your goal.

"Don't concern yourself with how you're going to achieve your goals. Leave that to a power greater than yourself. All you need to know is where you are going and the answers will come to you." - Dorothea Brandt

When stating your goals at this point, close your eyes and see yourself right there, in the room, achieving your goal.

Just Do It!
- Set your goals by following the CREATE criteria;
- Now close your eyes, take a few deep breaths, relax and count backwards from 5, 4, 3, 2, and 1.
- You are there in your goal. Imagine stepping into the end step, the evidence, your vision, your goal and experience what you see, what you hear, what you feel, what you say to yourself, how happy you are that you have achieved your goal, the goal that you set.
- Step right into it NOW and empower yourself with the success of achievement. Live it! Be it! Do it! Celebrate; your future goal is REAL!
- Stay in this place for a while and take a look around. Now slowly count back up from 1, 2, 3, 4 and 5 – you're very alert and back in the now.

Wow, how did that feel?

You now have the formula for CREATing real-life goals. It's time to implement it.

Your Turn.
Imagine a goal two weeks away; one month, and then three months away. Imagine that if you achieved those goals, how incredible that would be and how this success would move you closer towards your long-term, your ultimate goals.

Create your goal statements now. Use the C.R.E.A.T.E formula. Have fun and make them happen!

1. Two weeks away:

It is now

____

____

____

____

And I am/ I have

____

____

____

____

2. One month into the future:

It is now

____

____

____

____

And I am/ I have

____

____

____

____

3. Three months into the future:

It is now

____

____

____

____

And I am/ I have

____

____

____

____

HOW WAS THAT? – Continue to use this simple, yet **succinct and specific** template regularly for all your goals across:

- Your family goals
- Your relationship goals
- Your career and business goals
- Your health and wellbeing goals
- Your financial goals

Your everything...

PART 2

PASSION

Chapter 5
Dragon's Eyes - Passion

"A purpose is the eternal condition of success." - Bruce Lee

"Follow your passion" has become a well-known phrase. But what happens if you don't know what your passion is?

You may have asked yourself:

"What should I do with my life?'

"What is my passion?" or

"What is my purpose in life?"

Previously we addressed values and motivational drivers, and how they help you find your purpose. A most important element of this is knowing what you are passionate about, and how to find your passions. Without identifying your passion and gaining clarity on what that is, knowing your values or your motivators may be just rhetoric. Passion is the driving wheel.

If you want to be, content, happy, focused, and fulfilled, it is critical that you learn how to find your passion; embrace it, live it, and be guided by it otherwise you may think you have set your goals and action plans, but they may not fulfill you because they are not driven by your *'passion'* or *'life purpose.'* Therefore, you don't embrace them and associate into them fully to make any difference; you will be unlikely to achieve them. Even though you may enjoy what you do, on deeper self-discovery around your *purpose and passion,* you may find that you are passionate about something else altogether different than what you think you are.

How do I work it out? How do I know?

Plan to Win

Think clearly to gain clarity about your passion and purpose.

To help, ask yourself these basic questions:

What Empowers You?

What do you wish you could wake up and do every day?

For some people, it might be helping others. For others, it might be being able to express their creativity in their personal and professional life or being able to travel or spend time with their family.

Once you've really determined your ultimate goal in life, consider how you'll achieve it.

Start with a plan. How can you achieve your true purpose through your relationships, your career, and your values? Plan how you can make your personal and professional vision a reality.

After working with people of all ages from all over the world in international education and business, I believe that each of us is born with a unique life purpose. However, identifying, acknowledging, and honoring this purpose is perhaps the most important and also the most difficult action step successful people take. They take the time to understand what they are here to do – and then they pursue that with purpose and enthusiastic passion.

My Story on Finding My Passion and Purpose

For some, their purpose and passion in life is obvious and clear. Everybody comes into the world with a set of talents. Through support, encouragement, and persistent practice, those talents develop into skills.

Over time, many people from a young age realise they have natural talents, skills, and interests. They often drift towards vocations and search for experiences reflective of these in life.

Most of what I call my passions came easily to me. I just knew at some level. However, some of the realization, evidence, and implementation of these were not obvious until later on in my personal and professional life. I had many experiences and invested many years in learning how to master these skills. In other words, work is required, but suffering is not. If you are struggling and suffering, you are probably not living with purpose.

My parents shared that from about 4 years old, I would sit up the front of the room near the stage, near the band, completely oblivious to what was going on around me. I wouldn't move. I was in a zone, whilst my parents and friends enjoyed dancing and chatting with friends. I would just listen.

When I was old enough, I would search through my family record collection and play music of all types, as I was curious about all music, and I started to understand different styles of music; to be attracted to certain artists and so on. Around 8 years old I started to sing all the time. Outside on the backyard swing, walking around, in the house and sitting in the family car. I was a somewhat solitary child in my early years, content with being in music. Then I wanted to DO music – a natural step as I wanted to connect with my passion.

I joined a children's choir and could then see purpose. Learning the art of singing and being in a group was amazing and heaps of fun. Rehearsals and performances always made me feel good, even if I was nervous when asked to sing a solo – but having so much fun from the experience, I held onto that emotion and gave it my best shot. Success – belting out, although a bit shakily "I Saw Three Ships" at the annual Sunday School Christmas Concert.

When I was 10 years old, we were at a festival and I heard this great music and rhythm coming from what seemed to be from a group standing on the back of a truck. I walked over and was suddenly 4 years old again. I stood there for what seemed like hours focused on the trumpet player. Wow, I decided I wanted to do that and made a decision that somehow, I was going to play trumpet. A year later at the beginning of a new school year, I was sitting in music class and a special guest was introduced to us. We learned he was the local bandmaster. He talked to us about the local community brass band and then invited any of us to learn an instrument. That was it, my ears pricked-up, like a dog hearing its call for dinner. I couldn't wait for the end of the day to get home to tell my parents all about my day and seek permission to learn trumpet.

I wasn't worried about their response. Somehow, I knew they would be cool with it. Of course, yes, they were, and I started learning cornet the next week. I had attracted this opportunity through being focused, associated, and knowing that I would have the opportunity I had put out into the universe that day listening to that jazz trumpet player perform some incredible music on the back of that truck at the festival.

As the saying goes, the rest is history. At that time, I chose to be a performer and teacher of music, brass instruments, and a conductor– which was the core of what I did for most of my career. My passion has enabled me to perform with some of the greatest musicians there is or was; play in some of the most amazing venues around the world, and share my passion and skills with students of all ages in international schools and communities across five continents so far.

My passion was already there, I just needed to create the optimal opportunities to realise my passion, which became my purpose. My passion and purpose are to empower and inspire people, just like you. To assist you to be the best you can be in your personal life and in your career. To share with you tools and strategies, as I am doing in this book to give you confidence to explore your *"realms of pure potentiality,"* to introduce you to you, for you to get to know who you are, and what you want to do to live your passion and purpose. According to Deepak Chopra, your realm of pure potentiality is your home of intuition, balance, harmony, and bliss. Doesn't sound so bad, does it?

My other passion, martial arts, resembled my trumpet journey to become the next piece of solving the puzzle and chasing the dragon's tail. It further taught me about purpose and was a very inspiring motivational driver for me.

15 insights to help you find your life passion and explore your true purpose

1. What do you love to do? What comes easy to you?

We are all born with a deep and meaningful purpose that

we have to discover. Your purpose is not something you need to make up; it's already there. You will uncover it in order to create the life you want. Finding your passion could be easier than you think. Take some time to answer the following questions honestly. This could be the blueprint to start planning the rest of your life.

- What do you love to do?
- What comes easily to you?
- What subject could you read 100 books about without getting bored?
- What could you do for five years without getting paid?
- What would you spend your time doing with financial abundance to do anything?
- What three qualities do you most enjoy expressing in the world?
- What are three ways you most enjoy expressing these qualities? (For example, mine are inspiring and empowering people.)

Naturally, it does take work to develop your talents. For example, I am a musician and have been all my life, but I still have to practice regularly to keep in top playing form, but it feels natural. In music, all musicians, even the most gifted still has to practice, so the process of playing feels natural, automatic, without feeling like it's too great an effort; similar to rowing downstream rather than upstream. I also love to teach, to write, to coach and speak, to facilitate, to train, and to develop transformational seminars, workshops, and courses. I love to collaborate with other leaders, students, creative people of all ages to co-create new approaches to personal and professional work and to inspire aspiring leaders.

2. What qualities do you enjoy expressing the most?

First, ask yourself, *what are two qualities I most enjoy expressing in the world?* Mine are *inspiration* and *happiness.*

Second, ask yourself, *what are two ways I most enjoy expressing these qualities?* Mine are *inspiring* and *empowering* people.

I inspire people with the moving stories that I share in my workshops and speaking opportunities, and that I write about in my articles and books. I empower them by teaching them powerful strategies for success that they can apply in their personal and professional life.

3. Your Passion doesn't need to be your job.

You may have heard the saying "Anything that gets your blood racing is probably worth doing." There are many things worth doing that may not necessarily bring you money. You don't have to be great at something to be passionate about it. Some things just "feel great, feel right, you feel excited by," you like the emotional feeling you get; you are 'passionate' about a creative project, a type of music, a certain community service, for example.

4. What do you hate doing?

To further clarify your passions, make a list of tasks or activities that you absolutely do not like to do. Once you can see these, your true passion will become clearer. Now you have eliminated these options, create a list of people you are inspired by; those people that you 'want to be'; those you want to 'model' in your life or work. Ask yourself this question "Why do you want to be like them, why are you inspired by them and want to model them?" From this process list multiple individuals, look at the work they do and try those things. You might find your passion from this activity. This simple exercise will further help you gain clarity.

5. Your True Passion is not found overnight.

Inspiration may strike some people in an instant. Suddenly, without a doubt they know what they want to be and should be doing with their lives and why they are doing what they are doing. For others, it takes time and it takes work, but it does appear for you.

Your true passion is not found overnight, but is realized through a series of experiences - small or large, like it did for me in my story.

One of the best ways to help you find and understand your passion is to 'ask'. Yes, ask close friends and family, for example, what they think you should be doing with your life. If any of your friends and family have interests, hobbies, or passions that interest you, become involved, helping out or trying for yourself. Explore new activities, such as a new sport, learning a language, being creative with an activity or art. Explore new things as much as often as you can, be involved.

Spend 20 minutes each day thinking about what has interested you recently, maybe new ideas you have forgotten about for a while that appear for you to explore again, or any opportunities that you have seen and want to know more about. Read about it, watch some videos, talk to people about these, which will further educate you about them and maybe further fuel your passion for some of these activities that you didn't know you had?

6 What did you love doing when you were a child?

Did you like to draw pictures, read, sing, play sport? Try to remember the activities that you enjoyed during your childhood. Did you drift away from some of these as you became older and started to prioritise different things like what subjects to do at school, what to do at university or college to get a good job?

What hobbies did you enjoy before life became too busy? Do you think you would enjoy those activities now? Use these memories to help you find your true passion as an adult. Could you take back at least one of those activities or hobbies and commit to including them in your life more right now?

Recall all the fun and enjoyment you had from those activities now, think about how you could maybe improve your quality and fun for life right now by revisiting those. What a great feeling it would be to start drawing again or learning a musical instrument again.

Imagine that you are in your advancing years and somebody asks you - "What do you wish you had spent the last 20 to 30 years doing?" Think of this as if you were writing your memoirs and reflecting on your career, family, professional, and personal relationships. What did you not do as much of that you would have liked to?

7. Create your Life Purpose Statement

Take a few moments and write a description of what your perfect world would look like. For example, in my perfect world, everybody is fulfilling their highest potential, they feel they know themselves very well and they are **doing**, **being**, and **having** everything they want. They are living according to their **own vision**.

To create your life purpose statement, combine doing, being, and having into one statement. This will give you a clear idea of your purpose.

My statement is: *"In my ideal world I am inspiring and empowering people to live their highest vision in a context of self-motivation, wellbeing, happiness, confidence, and fulfillment."*

8. Inner Guidance - What is your heart telling you?

What if I told you that you have your own internal guidance system (IGS) – a powerful tool that's easy to use, that can help you get from where you are in life to where you want to be? It takes into account how you think, feel, and behave in order to be happy and successful in every situation you encounter. For example, if there is a difficult situation or conversation that you need to have, your IGS will lead you to the most satisfying and successful conclusion for you and everyone concerned. The problem is that most of us don't even know it's there. Perhaps you conceptually believe in an 'internal GPS', but you don't really understand it or how to access it.

Using the GPS metaphor when you get in your car and are heading to a specific destination, what is the first thing you input into your GPS? First, it finds your current location. Once it's determined where you are, it gives you directions to where you are heading. For the system to work, it simply needs to know your beginning location (A) and your end destination (B). The navigation system figures out the rest by the use of an onboard computer that receives signals from multiple satellites and calculates your exact position. Then it plots a perfect course for you. All you have to do from that point on is follow the instructions it gives you to reach your destination. If you take the time to understand how your own IGS functions, you can actually get to where you're going much faster than you would otherwise. As a result, your suffering is reduced and your joy and well-being is heightened.

For example, you want to feel rested. To continue with our GPS metaphor, try plugging "REST & REJUVENATE" into your inner guidance system. Then sit quietly for a moment while it computes and processes the results. Your inner guidance will inevitably tell you to take a power nap or sit for a brief meditation or reflection in order to feel rested. While you might think that lying on the couch in front of your favorite TV show might be the way to rest, your inner GPS will re-route you if you choose a less restorative path. It will always steer you down the most efficient route. Your inner guidance system knows which route is the best one to take to achieve your outcome.

Making Major Decisions using Your IGS

At times when making major decisions can be difficult or overwhelming, check in with your inner GPS when you're faced with choosing one path over another. The decision may be a life-path decision, a business decision, or a major financial decision. It doesn't matter what type, you just know in your 'gut' that the decision you make is a major decision which will have significant consequences.

6 steps to get you there:

1. **Look** at the fork in the road and identify the two options ahead of you. For example, it could be: *Do you take the job offer* or *Do you stay where you are?*

2. **Sit** with option one and daydream about what it would really feel like to go that route. If you're contemplating taking a job offer that would result in a pay increase and would require you to move across the country and leave family and friends behind, let yourself go down the mental and emotional pathway of what it would feel like to take the job. Try and associate into what it would feel like, look like, not only being at the job, but all the other circumstances that would come with the change.

3. **Notice** how do you feel in your chest and gut. Do you feel open, expansive, motivated, and excited? Or do you feel contracted, restrained and knotted up in your belly, like you're nervous, uncertain, and homesick?

4. **Imagine option two**. In this example, you're staying in your current job with the same salary, and nothing really changes.

5. **Notice again**: How does this second option feel for you, think deeper and deeper into your bones?

6. **Acknowledge** which option feels better in your heart space, *your intuition.* In which situation do you feel vital, enlivened, intrinsically motivated, and internally wide open? In which situation do you feel restricted, constricted, and tight? Trust your observations, your intuition, and remember that whatever expands you will make you happier.

The Ultimate Aim is Your Road to Happiness

For most of us, the ultimate destination on our GPS is happiness. Remember that every day you're either walking towards or away from happiness. It's never too late to change your route or destination. The clearer you are at the start, the less time you'll spend circling your destination. Circumstances will sometimes take you off-course. In these moments, remember the power of your own inner guidance system. When you slow down and check in with this sophisticated technology, you will always be able to find your way home.

9. Where do you want to go?

To decide where you want to go is by clarifying and staying focused on your vision, then lock in your destination through using tools and systems such as goal setting, affirmations, and visualization. Then start taking the actions that will move you in the right direction.

With every picture you visualize, you're *"inputting"* the destination you want to get to.

Every time you express a preference for something, you are expressing an intention.

A table by the window, front row seats at a concert, first-class flight tickets, a room with an ocean view, or a loving relationship. All these images and thoughts are sending requests to the universe.

If you stay out of its way, let the *'law of attraction'* work for you, without interrupting the process with negative self-talk, or a 'cocktail' of negative thoughts, doubts, and fears. Your inner GPS will keep unfolding the next steps along your route as you continue to move forward. In other words, the exact steps will keep appearing along the way in the form of internal guidance, creating ideas, and new opportunities.

10. Seek clarity about your Life Purpose

Once you are clear about what you want and why you want it and keep your mind constantly focused on it, the how will keep showing up. Your inner guidance system tells you when you are on or off course by the amount of fulfilment you are experiencing or happiness you are feeling. The things that bring you the greatest happiness are in alignment with your purpose and this will get you to where you want to go. When you embrace your goals, focus on them every day the universe will deliver. This is where the magic happens.

Ask yourself this question – "Where I am currently in my life?" Be honest, open, and reflect on what answers appear. Once you have clarity on this question, ask the ultimate question- "What do I want to do with my life?"

I asked myself this question. I was happy with what I was doing; immersed in education leadership, teaching in schools helping young people enjoy their learning, encouraging them and sharing tools with them and with colleagues; coaching and mentoring so they could be the best they could be in school and in life. So, all ok, or so I thought. From reflecting, trusting my intuition and doing some activities myself I knew I wanted to do more and I could. I wanted to share and have more input; to be on stage speaking to thousands of people, writing more books to get my ideas and tools out to the world, to be a 'game changer' for others; to be coaching more people, to have more autonomy in what I did and how I did it. I certainly knew the why I wanted to do it, and that's the most important first step. Getting the why clear.

I visualized, imagined, sought out opportunities to speak on stage at a conference, run workshops, create contacts that enabled consulting opportunities and so on, whilst still working in my regular role. The universe answered – messages started to come back from opportunities I had put out there, people started to contact me asking for my help, wanting advice and so on.

I am now a TED speaker, which I love, and from that opportunity came keynote speaking invitations at education and leadership conferences, invitations to run workshops, seminars and personal messages from aspiring leaders that wanted to know how to become education and school leaders; people that want to work with me as their coach, mentor or just to touch base and share ideas, their dreams and aspirations. "Of course, I would be happy to" is my response.

Think about where you would like to be?

If your life were perfect right now:

1. What would it look like?
2. What kind of job would you have?
3. Where would you be living?

By continually doing this exercise, you'll send powerful triggers to your unconscious mind to help you get there.

11. Your Passion Test

Developed by Chris and Janet Attwood, The Passion Test is a simple, yet elegant process. For the following statement, *"When my life is ideal, I am ___."* Choose the words to fill in the blank, which must be a verb.

You start by filling in the blank 15 times. When I went through the process, some of my statements looked like this:

- My life is ideal when I am helping people clarify and live their personal vision.
- My life is ideal when I am training or speaking to large groups of people.
- My life is ideal when I am helping people learn who they are.
- My life is ideal when people I work with identify their values.
- My life is ideal when I've assisted people to clarify what motivates them.
- My life is ideal when I am engaging students who want to be change makers in their life and community.
- My life is ideal when people feel inspired from

my speaking and coaching.

Similar to the previous activities for *'values'* and *'emotional drivers'* once you've created 15 statements, you identify the top 5 choices.

To do this:

- Compare statements #1 and #2 to identify which is most important.
- Take the top one of that comparison and decide whether it's more or less important than statement #3.
- Then take the winner of that comparison, and decide whether it's more or less important than statement #4, and so on until you've identified the passion that is most meaningful to you.
- Repeat the process with the remaining 14 statements to identify your second choice. Then repeat the process until you've pinpointed your top 5 passions in life.
- Next, create markers for each of your top five passions, so that you can look at your life and easily tell whether you are living that passion.

For example, my life goal is:

"When I'm helping people live their vision, based on identifying their values and motivational drivers to give them a focused and fulfilled life. I'm giving at least 20 speaking presentations and workshops per year for at least 10,000 people total. I'm writing at least 3 bestselling books per year and people want to meet me and are telling me,

'You've really empowered me to live my vision."

It's important you think big, don't apologise by thinking small as once you know what your passions are, and how your life will look when you are living it. You can create action plans to turn your dreams into reality.

Quick Quiz Based on The Passion Test

To get started, complete the following quiz as an introduction to *"The Passion Test."* To see what your responses to this quiz tells you about your living of the passionate life, go to: https://thepassiontest.com. Here you can take a short questionnaire online which will generate a profile for you, to help you with further clarification and understanding about you and finding your passions and purpose.

Are You Living a Passionate Life?

Answer the 7 questions below to reveal exactly how to discover your passions and create a life that you love. Taking this 7 question Passion Test Profile is a great start in determining if you are ready to get clarity about your passions and what is important to you. (Circle one)

1. I am excited about my life and turned on by the things I get to do each day.

- Never
- Rarely
- Sometimes
- Most of the time
- All the time

2. Others comment on how happy I am and what fun it is to be around me.

- Never
- Rarely
- Sometimes
- Most of the time
- All the time

3. I get upset and thrown off track when unexpected situations and circumstances arise.

- Never
- Rarely
- Sometimes
- Most of the time
- All the time

4. I am very clear about the top five passions in my life, those things that matter most to me.

- Not at all
- A little
- Somewhat
- Quite clear
- Crystal clear

5. I make decisions based on what will help me live my passions most fully.

- Never
- Rarely
- Sometimes
- Most of the time
- All the time

6. I spend my days doing things I love, surrounded by people I love.

- Never
- Rarely
- Sometimes
- Most of the time
- All the time

7. Life is confusing for me. I don't have a clear sense of direction in my life

- No sense of direction
- Very little sense of direction
- Some sense of direction
- Pretty clear sense of direction
- Very clear sense of direction

How did you do, what did you find out? Any patterns or common links in your responses?

12. When have you experienced great joy in your life?

Another way to help you identify your purpose is to conduct a reflection of when you experience great happiness and joy in an experience.

The process is to relive the experience. Make a list of all the times you've felt the greatest joy in your life. Choose one or two major joyful events and be specific in describing this major event.

Got it? Now find a comfortable place where you can relax with no distractions for about 30 minutes. Get in a comfortable position, maybe sitting or lying down.

1. Close your eyes, take a deep breath in...hold...breathe out... and relax. Take yourself into that joyful, happy event now.

2. Once you are there, look around – what sort of day was it; where were you, inside or outside? What was happening around you – the smells, was it warm or cold, raining or sunny? If outside, was the sky blue or gray? If inside, bright or dark? Just be in that location and relax now.

3. What were you doing, why have you chosen this event that made you so happy? Go into that event...You are back in that event...now. Breathe in and out slowly, relaxing and happy. Feel the big silly grin on your face and your whole body simply feeling so joyful because you are here... in that event right now.

4. As you are enjoying this time, why did you like it so much, what emotions were you feeling? How did you feel? Ask yourself what can I learn about my passions and life purpose from this

event...just stay in this moment and relax...keep smiling and feeling absolute joy. Then when you are ready, slowly open your eyes and come back into the now.

5. Welcome back, now with paper and a pen, write down the feelings you just experienced; why did re-visiting that event make you feel so happy; why did you choose that event amongst all events you noted down before doing the process. What made you passionate about wanting to experience that event again? Write the words, keywords, descriptions and feelings down.

How was that? What do you now know about your life passions and purpose? How might you be able to take those findings into your life starting now?

Since we know that joy and happiness are drivers as part of your internal guidance system, telling you when you are on course, you can determine a lot about your life purpose from completing this joy review.

13. Finding Purpose. A Story!

Music and Passion: As a young conductor, I remember the feeling of joy, and with some anxiety, when I was asked by a well-known international composer if I would conduct the premiere performance of his new work for Choir and Orchestra at a prestigious International Music Festival. With a huge smile on my face and a nervous exciting energy, I recall walking into the first rehearsal with the Orchestra and Choir. Over 100 people standing and sitting in position right there in front of me, in a wonderful performance hall, probably as excited and maybe as anxious as I was. We were there to share our skills and energy, whilst connecting with each other to bring all of the parts together, and hear, for the first time, what this composition was going to sound like.

I took my place in front of this massed choir and orchestra, smiling with a focused willingness to give all I could to all of these musicians; they knew I was with them all the way and supported them on this journey we were about to take together. With baton in my right hand, my left hand raised, I invited these talented people to come with me. With an expanded awareness of everyone in front of me and a warm heart I gestured them to start to play. The sound that came back at me was incredible, moving, and beautiful. My heart smiled and so did I. We were on our way.

On finding purpose is when I am teaching, and when I am inspiring and empowering people to go for their dreams and to have more love, joy, and abundance in their lives.

14. Align your goals with your Life Purpose and Passions

We all have skill-sets, talents, and interests that tell us what we're supposed to be doing. Once you know what your life purpose is, organize your activities around it. Everything you do should be an expression of your purpose. If an activity or goal doesn't fit that formula, don't work on it. For example, aligning with your purpose is most critical when setting professional goals. When it comes to personal goals, you have more flexibility.

If you want to learn to play an instrument or surf, go ahead and do so. If your goal is to be healthy and fitter by losing weight, move ahead with confidence. Nurturing yourself emotionally, physically, and spiritually will make you more energized, resilient, and motivated to live your purpose.

In your professional life, don't ignore the signs that maybe it is not right for you. An easy sign for this is if you dread Monday mornings and have no motivation to 'jump out of bed' and head off to work; instead you count the hours and minutes until the weekend. This may be a sign that it's time to follow your heart and pursue the work you long to do.

15. Moving towards your true-Life Purpose

Once you have gained more clarity about your purpose, you don't need to change everything in your life at once to say you have achieved it. Instead, just move towards it, little by little.

To do this, start by living your purpose a little more fully every day. Pay attention to how your self-talk has positively changed, and the feedback you receive from others. What is it telling you? Reflect on what results you are producing in your life. Also the most obvious one. Pay attention to how you are feeling.

As a checklist, regularly ask yourself these questions:

Am I where I want to be?
- Have I accomplished all I thought you would by 'now' – the date you committed to?
- Am I enjoying the lifestyle, travel, weekends, and leisure pursuits I've always dreamed of?
- Do I want a more fulfilling career or business?
- Could my relationships be deeper, more rewarding, and more meaningful?

Note to Self: Be decisive, commit to where you are, why and how you are going to get to where you want to be.

3 non-decisive personality traits to be aware of for your success

1. Is this you? - the most uncommitted response - "I have to think about it."

Do you overthink? Overthinking leads to no decision 'freeze-frame'. Very quickly after a long session of overanalyzing, all you want to do is find distraction. You know- 'sleep', watch TV, eat and so on to forget you even thought about it. This is a recipe for disaster when it comes to making smart choices. Of course, you should give things thought and avoid making irrational and impulsive decisions you may regret later. But, there's a difference between seriously needing to weigh your options and using "I have to think about it" as an excuse to buy time and avoid a decision.

Every opportunity has an expiration date and if you spend too much time being indecisive or too scared to give a definite answer, or even too scared to ask for what you want, you'll miss out on moments that can positively impact your personal life and your career.

2. Is this you? – the humble, modest type - "I don't want to sound arrogant."

If you worry about sounding arrogant, rarely take credit for your work, and constantly say things like "I don't like bragging about myself," you may be guilty of being too modest. While those sentences may make you feel like a humble team player, your unwillingness to speak up about how valuable you are signals to other people that you lack value and confidence. When you give yourself permission to apologise or 'downplay' your success, you give others permission to overlook you. This is not arrogance.

In your career, for example, no matter how ambitious you feel, how qualified you may be, how hard you work, or how helpful you are; if you fail to clearly articulate your value to others, it will hinder your opportunities for growth and leadership. Your fear of talking about yourself can hold you back from promotions and job offers, for example. It's time you put the "I don't want to sound arrogant" speech in the bin for good and learn how to gracefully and confidently advocate for yourself.

3. "I'll do it later."

How often do you play this card? Some people may interpret procrastination on the surface as another word for 'laziness'. On a deeper level, procrastination is the product of fear and uncertainty. For example, have you ever had a moment when you knew you wanted to do something, or your spouse or children asked you to commit to something, and you put it off and forgot about it, or stumbled upon your dream job, got excited, and instead of applying, immediately 'procrastinated' and decided to do it later? Have you ever been given the opportunity to work on a complex project you've never done before, and for some reason, it always ends up on the bottom of your to-do list?

Procrastination is born when you don't want to do something because you're scared of the outcome, or when you don't want to start something because you don't know all the steps to complete it. To break this "I'll do it later" mentality, when you hear the words about to roll out of your mouth, get clear on whether **fear or uncertainty** is holding you back from moving forward. Then, **address those issues** directly, either by tackling your fear or getting additional direction, so you can finally **take action**.

PART 3

CERTAINTY AND DECISIVENESS

Chapter 6
Dragon's Wings – The Power of Certainty and Decisiveness

"If a man will begin with certainties, he shall end in doubts; but if he will be content to begin with doubts, he shall end in certainties." — Francis Bacon

What is certainty?
"We need to have complete certainty that things will work out, not because we are righteous or wise, but because of the time, the effort, the prayers, and the tools we are using. From the moment we are given awareness about some bigger picture or mission, we have to have complete focus on what to do to get to that place." -Yehuda Berg

You must know your core, which always remains the same despite other things changing. This core is not our emotions, thoughts, beliefs, or our bodies. It is the realisation of something which is the basis of all. It is the essence of who we and everyone is. It is knowing and living in the inherent oneness of life. Everything is uncertain and changing, only the background, the essence where it takes place doesn't change a bit. Certainty is not a thing; certainty is a feeling, closely affiliated to a feeling of truth.

It takes courage to move from the known to the unknown, but the price of growth is a sacrifice of certainty. Life can be difficult and uncertain, especially when faced with the prospect of change. Although change is often the key that will positively alter the path of our lives, we shy away from it for fear of leaving behind our comfort zones and entering into the unknown.

Certainty assumes faith. If you are certain you can do something, you have faith that you will. If you doubt you can do something, this lack of faith will ultimately lead to underachievement. Henry Ford said, *"If you think you can, you will. If you think you can't, you won't."*

I discovered the power of certainty. The sky was blue, it was a fantastic warm sunny Melbourne day and I was preparing for my college trumpet performance recital. I had been practicing hard and was on a tram to my teacher's house for a lesson. The day was grand and I was looking forward to sharing with my teacher the rewards of my practice sessions. My recital was in two weeks. I also had some questions as to why I was constantly not able to perform certain sections of a couple of the pieces I was preparing.

I arrived at my destination, grabbed a take-away coffee from a nearby vendor, and felt the sun on my back as I walked to his house. Life was pretty good, I thought.

I sat down with my teacher, and following some banter and friendly conversation, we got into work. We played through some of my repertoire, feeling good. Before we were about to tackle these two pieces, I was having trouble with, I thought it was a good time to ask some questions about the difficulty I was having with the upper register requirements of this music–to play high notes on the trumpet is athletic in itself. I figured he would advise me with what I could do to 'nail' these sections. Each time I arrived at this section, I couldn't play it or I made some kind of interesting sound that I would be stretched to call musical. A few attempts went by; we stopped, we talked, and tried some different techniques and approaches to see if it helped. Our 60-minute lesson had already gone over as we were spending time on these sections. I was getting quite mentally and physically tired and frustrated. I wanted **certainty** that I could play this music. Self-doubt crept in, second-guessing myself – the usual mental games our mind plays on us when we feel uncertain about something. What was I to do?

My teacher presented me with a small mirror and asked me to take a good look at what was going on when I tried to play these notes. So, with my trumpet placed on my lap, I played –went through the motions physically of what my embouchure (facial muscles and lips) was doing. As we watched in the mirror, we discovered what it wasn't doing.

Self-doubt and uncertainty enveloped me as my teacher said the words, "You are going to need to change your playing embouchure, or you're always going to be limited in achieving your goals – you will never be as proficient as you need to be to perform well on trumpet".

My heart sank, and he kept talking –it was all a blur by that stage, what was he saying – I didn't care. According to my self-talk, I had failed as a musician; I had to be a beginner again, learn all over again; my passion was extinguished at that point. As I started to wake from my stupor, I realized my recital was in two weeks – that wasn't going away. As I 'came back', I heard "it will take 3 to 6 months of daily exercises and a different kind of practice routine, but then you will play anything." "Play anything" – my ears pricked up. Three to six months' sacrifice to be able to play 'anything'. I believe blood started to return to my face and at that point, I made a decision that to achieve certainty I had to do this, I would do this, it was going to be fine – better than fine. I stepped up, and decided to rid my mind of uncertainty, replace it with this challenge and my mind was made up that I would do this and be a better musician than I had ever been. Yes, it would mean not playing for a while – at least not the music I was used to and that's ok.

"Knowing others is intelligence; knowing yourself is true wisdom. Mastering others is strength; mastering yourself is true power." — Lao Tzu, *Tao Te Ching*

Thoughts on Certainty
1. Does certainty give happiness? To be certain is mostly just trying to see if the image of something fits with what you think you want it to be.
2. To know something is "right' for you isn't something you decide, it's something you create.
3. Life is not a straight line from here to there.
4. Many people don't know what they want anyway.
5. A huge problem is we don't know how to be comfortable in uncertainty. This is a problem because the other side of uncertainty is potential. How do we identify it and achieve it?
6. What is "meant to be' is not something you figure out, it's something you realise after the fact.
7. The things that are most "right" for you will make you feel more uncomfortable than not.
8. Your life actually moves forward when you let yourself experience what you didn't plan for. The uncertainty of certainty.

9. The desire for certainty is ultimately a fear of your emotions.

10. The only thing you can only ever truly be certain of is whether or not you are in the moment, appreciating what you have, while you have it. Certainty is a feeling.

Certainty: Is it possible to be absolutely certain of anything?

"I fear not the man who has practiced 10,000 kicks once, but I fear the man who has practiced one kick 10,000 times."
Bruce Lee

An aim for you might be to have certainty in your ability, or in the ability of others. For example, in your team or your professional relationships. Yes, we can be absolutely certain of many things, most of which we might not care about. For things that we care about deeply, we are far more likely to mistakenly feel certain of things that we cannot possibly know. We want to know what will happen next. Yet we can't. Our desire to know is so intense that we often convince ourselves we have figured *it* out, whatever *it* is. We think we know what will happen next, only to be gravely disappointed when something else happens due to untold variable factors. This is the cause of the sense that we can't be absolutely certain of anything - even though we can be certain of some things.

How long can we live without certainty?

Being certain of anything does **not** always mean it's good for you. Most of the time, it's actually something that might put you and/or other people at disadvantage. You really can't be too certain about anything at all. We are in the age of a lot of scientific discovery, technological explosion, and philosophical turn around in human history. For example, thanks to technology and internet, people of today can do and *know so much more* than ever before. At the tip of your finger, or click of a mouse, you can actually know what you didn't know, and realize how much you didn't know on a daily basis.

Human history will show you that certainty had been a kind of staple of our society. The entirety of human civilization had been built around finding the *absolute truth* of life, universe, and everything in between—that of course, would require certain amount of certainty to be manifested properly. The search for *absolute certainty* is one of the biggest things holding humanity back.

Activity: Have you experienced certainty?

If you don't know, or maybe can't recall what it feels like to feel an absolute sense of certainty, recall a time, or an event in your past which created a feeling of certainty to you. Ask yourself these questions:

How did it feel?

How did you know it was certainty?

Was it an emotional reaction or a sensory experience?

Imagine why you would feel like if you were able to feel an

absolute sense of certainty in various aspects, or decisions in your personal and professional life.

The Power of Certainty

Creating a sense of certainty and commitment that you can achieve whatever you desire is powerful and life-changing. However, if you allow fear and doubt to take over, they become an enemy that can destroy all possibilities. They control you, make you lower your expectations and settle for less, not achieving your goals. On the other hand, when you summon your courage to conquer these enemies to success, you open the doors to high achievement with **certainty** and self-assuredness. A lack of certainty can stop us in our tracks. If we don't feel certain inside about what we want or what we need to do to get there, then we give up before we even begin. However, we can create a sense of certainty and develop it like a muscle. The more we use it, the better we'll get. **Certainty is a key** to unlocking what's holding us back.

When ideas are taking hold in your mind, there's a battle between your conscious and unconscious mind. Your conscious mind might want something, but your unconscious mind might not believe you. When there is this conflict, ideas lose strength, and do not enter your unconscious, so you'll lack a sense of certainty. You won't feel it in your deepest core.

When you don't feel a sense of certainty, you won't take action. Makes sense. Why bother if it won't work? When you don't have certainty, you are likely to go into *doing nothing* mode because when you don't have a sense of certainty about the outcome or how you'll get there, you stand still. You fall into *analysis paralysis*, or you put things off, or you do things half-heartedly and non-committed.

When you decide on your outcome and you create a plan to get there, you increase your confidence. You also increase your clarity, as you figure out what specifically you want to achieve, and how you'll get there. You take massive action. And massive action is how you make things happen.

Tony Robbins - *"If you decide that you will do something, and start to plan towards it, you create confidence. If you resolve within yourself the sense of absolute certainty that 'I'm going to do this!' and then you* **start to build a plan**-*something extraordinary happens. You begin to develop the certainty you can actually achieve it."*

To develop your sense of real certainty, make it a habit of finding models and reference examples that inspire you to what's possible. Learn what they do that helps them achieve their amazing results. In my experience, if other people can do it, you can, too.

How can we be sure of certainty?
You can't always be sure of anything 100% of the time. If by being sure of certainty, you mean a kind of *absolute* certainty, then I will say **you can't,** and that's fine some of the time. One should not be obsessed with being absolutely certain about everything.

Certainty is similar to another kind of very strong notion - perfection. In a practical sense, being certain of anything or to strive for perfection can be a very unproductive mindset that would often lead to disappointment. In one sense, certainty is one form of perfection—it is the perfection of knowledge of something, sometimes to the point that no other possibility is allowed especially when what you're looking at is a case for *absolute certainty.*

Why do we seek certainty?

If we don't mind what will happen next in our lives, we would have no reason to be concerned, stressed, or worried. Although this sounds like the ideal ticket to emotional freedom, most of us cannot help it and do care what happens next in our lives. Why, because as we see in Maslow's Hierarchy of Needs, it is in our natural state as human beings to care about, to want security, wellbeing, health, safety and so on, we want certainty! We want to make sure that the things we want to happen actually do happen and that is where our need for certainty begins. Yet, we can't control everything and life is filled with twists and turns; sometimes our efforts to secure certainty leave us far from the life that we desire. We don't like to feel like this. We don't like to feel *uncertainty.*

Uncertainty feels, to the brain, like a threat to your life. Our "need to know" can become the foundation for every choice that we make. Our search for certainty affects how we face life. For example, in our career we may have a preference towards a particular job. We just feel it will give us certainty with a guaranteed future or pay grade. We favor the view to suit our goals, and our 'certainty;' we choose relationships that feel secure, or engage in activities we know and feel comfortable with, with certainty. Sometimes these decisions work out great, however often we are ignoring new opportunities, inhibiting our creativity and true desires for the sake of certainty. Courage and risk are needed to achieve certainty. If we take a risk, and find the courage to face the unknown, we can examine new ideas, go places we never expected to go, or develop positive and unique relationships.

When you can't predict the outcome of a situation, an alert goes to the brain to pay more attention. Think about someone you have spoken to a few times by phone, but never met or seen a picture of. You feel a mild uncertainty about them, yet even this tiny uncertainty seems to alter your interactions: notice how differently you interact once you know what that person looks like. Uncertainty is like an inability to create a complete map of a situation. With parts missing, you're not as comfortable as when the map is complete. The brain likes to think ahead and picture the future, mapping out how things will be. It gets complex when there's two or more possible outcomes. Imagine expecting a colleague to phone you at 3pm. It's now 3.06pm. You automatically start to try to predict two futures: if he calls now, will he apologise? You start to question and doubt - What made him late? Is he okay? And if he doesn't call, what should you now do with your spare hour? Flitting between these different ideas is exhausting, your brain wants to settle on one idea, not keep shifting between possible futures. Your brain wants certainty. Scientific American Mind magazine goes so far as to call this an 'information addiction' explaining the chemistry of this addition in an October 2009 article. It's all about the burst of dopamine we get when a circuit is completed. It feels good - but that doesn't mean it's good for us all the time.

We automatically avoid uncertainty which is why any kind of change can be hard. We prefer things we know over things that might be more fun, or better for us, but are new and therefore uncertain. It explains why we prefer the certainty of focusing on problems and finding answers in data from the past, rather than risking the uncertainty of new, creative solutions.

How can you create absolute certainty of belief?

When the legendary Muhammad Ali passed away, the world was treated to much of the television footage of Ali claiming he was the king of the world before each fight. He demonstrated an unshakeable belief in himself. He showed qualities we could all learn from.

I've learned over the years that when you have absolute certainty on your side, you become far more capable than without it. The ability to believe with the conviction of all your body and mind will help you perform at your best. So, the very **belief** that you can do it makes it more possible.

How do you do this? Very simply...you imagine it being possible over and over again. You act with every cell of your soul that it's possible...over and over again. You train your mind to see it again and again. However, don't *beat yourself up*. Look at it from both sides; consider what will happen if it doesn't work out and commit to embracing that. This provides you with a sense of freedom from worry or stressing about it. Instead, you know no matter what happens, you will handle it. Act from a position of strength. Then, return back to vividly seeing yourself winning and succeeding over and over again. By investing mental energy in the things you want to manifest, you become vigilant with your mind and refuse to dwell on anything but success. Doing this creates a sense of strength and certainty that can be immensely powerful. Being **certain** is important to **make decisions** in life, or none of us would be able to be convinced to do anything.

Be decisive! Make the decisions to master your mind.

"One cannot accomplish things simply with cleverness. One must take a broad view. It will not do to make rash judgments concerning good and evil. However, one should not be sluggish. It is said that one is not truly a samurai if he does not make his decisions quickly and break right through to completion" - from Hagakure, The Book of the Samurai

The Sage of *The Karate Kid* Sensei Miyagi expresses decisiveness this way:

Miyagi: *Walk on road, hm? Walk left side, safe. Walk right side, safe. Walk middle, sooner or later [makes squish gesture] get squish just like grape.*

Miyagi: *Here, karate, same thing. Either you karate do "yes" or karate do "no." You karate do "guess so," [makes squish gesture]*

Miyagi: *Just like grape. Understand?*

Certainty + Decisiveness = True Certainty, True Success

Life can often feel overwhelming, especially when we face many options, pending decisions, and countless unknowns.

Making a decision can seem daunting, and even scary, when you consider the long list of impacts your decision will have. You may feel clouded and confused as your mind starts to question, second-guess the decision, analyse the potential consequences of the decision. It can be easy to get caught in the mayhem of reaching a conclusion. This is not unusual, just trust yourself that you will find making a decision is as simple, or as complicated, *as you choose it to be.*

Our life path is shaped by the decisions we make in every moment. If we are not conscious in the decisions we make, then we feel as if we are endlessly drifting in an 'unconscious bubble', feeling helplessly hopeful, yet afraid to face the unknown. Burst the bubble, take control, and decide to be decisive. Trust yourself and your decisions. Step up and be decisive.

"Show me your position....you want your back doing the hard labor, you're holding - never hold...your muscles tense up when you hold...pull the string back to the centre of your chin and release...never hold..."but I have to aim"...never aim...your eye knows where it wants the arrow to go...trust your eye" - Game of Thrones

The perceived ability to make a clear decision comes with the choice and belief that you are Decisive. Clarity has power and making an unquestionable decision gives you energy. This absolute energy will attract the resources and support you need to carry out that decision.

When you are clear and sharp on your decision, others will not second guess you. Being decisive is simply a mindset, not magic; a mental attitude that comes with practice and persistence.

Does it sometimes seem like you're the only one who doesn't know how to make decisions? When you're not confident about making a decision, it's tempting to just avoid them altogether. Regardless of the root of your indecisiveness, you are likely to feel frustrated and powerless. You can implement some approaches to thinking differently to make things better, which can assist you to stop being indecisive. Your indecisiveness may not always be about your decision-making about you, but why you make decisions. For example:

1. **Are you trying to please other people?** Referring back to Maslow's hierarchy of basic human needs, consider *Significance*. Are you thinking that if you let others get their own way, they'll like you more? Do you find yourself in the habit of letting everyone else go first when it comes to making a decision that you can almost lose the ability to make your own choice?

2. **Following some bad choices do you feel disappointed?** At an unconscious level, your self-talk is encouraging you to **lose faith in your own judgment.**

3. **Does choice confuse you?** Society presents plentiful options. Whenever you want to decide what to eat for dinner, where to go on holiday, or what pair of shoes to buy, do you feel bombarded by potential outcomes, is it all just too hard? Working out how to make up your mind can be that much harder when

you're overwhelmed.

Considering some of these basic factors that influence your ability to be decisive, let's further explore how to stop being indecisive. Focus and reflect on the following straightforward and powerful techniques that you can use when learning how to make good decisions. With committed application of these in your daily routine, you will likely start seeing results straight away.

7 keys to moving from Indecisiveness to Decisiveness

The following are techniques I use to gain clarity. I have found them to be helpful in helping me become more decisive. See how they work for you.

1. Believe in yourself

You are Decisive! The more you tell yourself, and indicate to others, that you are *indecisive,* the more difficult it will be to be *decisive.* This attitude doesn't help you if you really want to commit to making fast and firm decisions.

2. Tune into You and Your Emotions

To move towards being a decisive person, one of the first things you need to do is stop over-thinking things. The more you overthink, the more you analyse everything. Learn to trust your intuition – Trust Your Gut! Intuition is an amazing monitor of feelings and emotions towards making decisions. If you work on tuning into your emotions more accurately, you'll develop finely developed intuition that will help you to make choices without overanalyzing. Being more emotionally aware can help you a great deal.

Activity

How to start tuning in to your emotions and trusting your intuition

- Try time-limiting your decisions. For example, make a list of your options, then let your gut tell you how to rate them from 1 to 10. Go with the highest rated choice, and notice how often this is right.
- Prove and experience the trust of your intuition by making a list of five times in life when your gut was right.
- Enrich and tune in to your awareness by keeping a daily journal and reflecting on your emotions. You will be surprised what you learn about yourself and your 'emotional buttons'. Start with a page-a-day. Schedule time in your day to engage with your emotions and intuition through doing these journal entries. Look for patterns. It will help you tap into reflective and intuitive capacities that may have been dormant or that you have ignored.

3. Visualize Possible Outcomes

Visualize yourself as a confident and decisive person who is able to make quick and firm decisions. Try it now. Go ahead, close your eyes, see yourself in decisive action. "What do you look like on the outside?" "How do you feel on the inside?"

When figuring out how to make difficult decisions

visualization takes you closer to the reality of the different choices you have. This, in turn, can make the right choice much clearer. It can also offer some much-needed reassurance that a decision isn't as significant or ominous as you might have thought. If you already have some experience with visualization, you'll find this technique very easy. However, if the concept of visualization, or the visualization process is new to you, try this.

Activity

Simply close your eyes and breathe deeply until you feel relaxed. Then, using the power of your imagination, *'associate'* yourself into all the possible choices before you, one at the time. Notice what each scenario feels like, looks like. How does it make you feel; where do you feel it in your body? If the feeling for example is in your upper chest and you feel a strange pressure or shortness of breath, write down why you think that scenario makes you feel that way. Maybe there is a degree of fear associated with making a decision around that. That's ok, just reflect on it through writing it down and the feelings you associate with it. Another scenario, you may feel it in your solar-plexus area. It may be a feeling of good energy – like your smiling inside. You may even start laughing or have a huge grin on your face. That's ok. Trust your intuition. It may be telling you to move forward on that decision, whatever it might be. Trust your emotions and intuition.

If this kind of creative visualization doesn't work that well for you, or you are not comfortable with it, it doesn't matter, there are other approaches. For example, drawing a mind map is another way of visualizing decisions, just in a more linear and logical way. Using different colored pens and symbols illustrate the pros and cons of each choice. This process can really help you to make sense of the information that has been racing around your head, but don't fall into the trap of overanalyzing. Even if you only perceive a limited set of options, you are never so limited. Expand the possibilities by considering your hidden assumptions and creatively brainstorm other solutions.

4. Be Brave to Take Action

Don't be afraid to make mistakes. You will get better at evaluating situations, information and your emotions the more you do it. Let the fears subside.

When moving towards a decisive lifestyle, it's important to remember that you can learn what works, and also learn from mistakes.

1. Don't become indecisive about the process of battling indecision! Learning what works for you is a process of trial and error that relies on your willingness to experiment. When you choose to try different techniques, you will be able to assess what pushes you towards better, more effective decision-making.

2. Do make a habit of pushing yourself out of your 'comfort zone'. Take action in all areas of your personal and professional life and feel safe in the knowledge that you can make something good out of every possible outcome. Even when things don't turn out as you'd expected or would have liked, this provides fresh opportunities for learning. Often, it is the lessons we learn from so-called mistakes that end up leading us to a better life later on. Start small, and slowly allow yourself to

become more open to trying new things. Proving your own willingness, resilience, versatility, and adaptability are some of the best ways to prove to yourself that indecision is not necessary and that you have the power to handle whatever comes your way.

Learn to listen to your instincts. Have **faith** and **trust** your 'gut'. Pay close attention to what your inner voice is telling you. Recognize that there are no 'bad' decisions. Have faith that no matter which decision you choose, that there is a wonderful lesson behind it, and that you will benefit from it, regardless of its potential outcome. Action beats inaction.

5. Take Your Time

There are various reasons why you should sometimes set a time limit when making decisions. There are some scenarios where more time is better. For example, there is much research that suggests if you take a short break from thinking about your choices, you can end up making a better decision. It's true you may feel an urgency sometimes about having to make your decision immediately which can create anxiety. This anxiety, in turn, makes it almost impossible to focus on a choice. Stop, relax, reflect, and put it aside for a while. Go for a walk, do something completely different and pleasurable, away from your decision making. Return fresh, clear headed, and confident. Keeping in mind that for some decisions you can make them quickly, on a tight deadline. Depending on the scenario –reminding that it is easy to procrastinate and overanalyze when you don't need to. Make some fast decisions. These will become easier over time. Start with making small decisions like "What are you going to do for dinner?" "How shall you spend the weekend?" – All good practice – Persistent practice makes perfect.

6. Learn to trust yourself

Pushing beyond indecisiveness is also about finding your unique strengths and then figuring out how you can use those to help the decision-making process. Most people who struggle with indecision can find it hard to keep an awareness and focus on their strengths.

Activity - Who are you right now?

List at least five strengths you think you have, more if you can. When you are preparing your list or if you find it difficult, think of the strength's others have highlighted about you. For example, you are creative, great with words, a talented writer, an inspiring communicator, warming caring nature, always optimistic, funny and so on. Then, think of at least one way that each strength could be used to help you be better in your decision-making. For example, optimism can be used to convince yourself that you can survive any outcome of a decision. Your creativity to draw or design a picture may help you next time you are trying to make a choice – make a decision.

7. Now -Think out loud and make a decision.

- Find a fresh notebook.
- Clearly define the question at the top of the page, write down your options and assumptions, followed by any other thoughts or concerns you have. Put all your thoughts down as they enter your mind. Don't think

about it, or edit it, just write it all down.

- It doesn't matter if your thoughts are unclear or do not flow, just keep going.
- Take a look at your page now. What have you written down? WHY have you written down what you have?
- Decisiveness comes with the Decision that you are Decisive. Decide today.

PART 4

MINDSET AND MODELLING

Chapter 7
Dragon's Mind - Changing Your Mindset

"A man is literally what he thinks. This might be a shocking statement, but everything is a state of mind" - Bruce Lee

"Nothing is impossible. The word itself says, 'I'm possible.'"
- Audrey Hepburn

Many people I meet have a mindset that is totally working against them. They know what they want, they're constantly trying to pursue that goal, and making a great effort to achieve it, but never really reaching it. Let's unpack our mindset, see if we can work it out, and learn some tools to help us to take control of it, so we can achieve what we want across all areas of our career, relationships, health, money – our life generally.

How do we find success by changing our mindset? What do you mean by mindset? Is it how we think, how we learn, how we make decisions, how we feel, why we do what we do?

It is all those things as you are what you think.

Consider some common day-to-day beliefs that concern you, or you spend time in your day dreaming about; or you make detailed lists about every New Year. Beliefs like:

- It's hard for *me* to lose weight.
- *I'm* not good with numbers.

- *I'm* not a natural athlete.
- *I'm* not creative.
- *I'm* a procrastinator.
- *I'll* never be happy in my job
- I'll never be able to buy nice things
- And so on...

What is something you notice about these belief statements? They all start with "I" or "me." 'Drum Roll please'... 'Aha moment' is here...Ok, all jokes aside. These beliefs will happen as 'You are what You Think." You live your life how you think your life. To change your life, to achieve what you want, you need to change your mindset and the 'self-talk' you use every day, even unconsciously as you go about your daily tasks. This is called a 'fixed mindset' around these thoughts.

I can guarantee, and many others before me, that those fixed mindsets will lead you to avoid experiences where you might feel like a failure. As a result, you don't learn as much, you don't try as hard (in those areas) and it's harder to get better.

What can you do about this? Relax, there is not one single reason why we struggle to achieve our goals or to break bad habits or be able to excel in our work life and find our passions or purpose. More often than not, the biggest challenge is between your ears. Yes, your MIND – your MINDSET.

Your mind is incredibly powerful. Depending how you use it can be your friend or your foe - a double-edged sword.

Remember we all have stories that we write in our game of life. In these stories you tell you the beliefs you have about yourself. The way you talk to yourself can either be the limiting factor holding you back, or the key to blossoming in your life goals. You can change your mindset towards what you want to achieve rather than what you don't want. That is, often in our use of language, in how we talk to others, our self-talk, how we think about things is in an 'away from motivation' rather than a 'towards motivation'.

For example, "I will never be able to lose weight" is an away from motivation. How, the keywords in this thought, this self-talk are **"I will never** be able to **lose weight."** Let's flip that thought to what you 'do want', not what you 'don't want' – **"I am healthy, energetic**, feel, and look great." Say to yourself the first statement – how do you feel? Now say the second statement – how do you feel? Hopefully you feel much more positive. Imagine saying that each morning before you start your day how much better you will feel.

What happened? You just changed your mindset around weight and feeling great. The more you use positive affirmations like this, and apply it to beliefs you may have around different things, your mind will get more and more used to these positive thoughts and before long you, (your mind) will attract what you want into your life, not what you don't want.

Try this activity
Think about three things you want to change, or you feel you have a negative or an away-from thoughts or beliefs around. Got it!

Step 1: Write what you don't want, in words that motivate you *away from* what you want.

Step 2: Now create a statement that motivates you *towards what* you do want.

Example:
1. I am never able to afford to go on a holiday overseas. *(away from motivation)*
2. I am grateful and happy that I can confidently pay for my amazing holiday to Italy next April. *(towards motivation)*.

Put this positive statement into your daily routine and you may be surprised what happens.

This is a very simple way to alter your mood, your mindset, your results; by using positive towards motivation language, and self-talk every day to move towards your goals and aims. This is an example of a growth mindset. You see, the unconscious mind doesn't decide for you what will happen. *'It'* only processes what you feed it day after date – your thoughts, doubts, celebrations, happiness, success ... or not! You decide. You do, based on your self-talk.

According to Stanford University researcher Carol Dweck, the difference may come down to your mindset, or more specifically, whether you embrace a "fixed" or a "growth" mindset.

Dweck describes the difference between these two mindsets, and how they impact your performance.

"In a fixed mindset, students believe their basic abilities—their intelligence, their talents—are just fixed traits. They have a certain amount and that's that, and then

their goal becomes to look smart all the time and never look dumb. In a growth mindset, students understand that their talents and abilities can be developed through effort, good teaching and persistence. They don't necessarily think everyone's the same or anyone can be Einstein, but they believe everyone can get smarter if they work at it.

Can you see the relationship to your life? **Believe it or not,** most of us are guilty of having a fixed mindset—at least in certain situations. And that can be incredibly dangerous and destructive because a fixed mindset can prevent skill development and growth, which can be disastrous for health and happiness over time.

How can you change the things you believe about yourself, eliminate your fixed mindset, and actually achieve your goals?

Although the way to change your mindset looks and sounds simple, like most change, it does not necessarily mean it is easy to do. For example, consider skills development. Skill is something you can learn, develop, practice, cultivate, and implement, rather than something you are born with. You can become more creative, athletic, more intelligent, artistic, and more successful by focusing on the process of developing skills needed rather than just the outcome.

For example:

- Instead of worrying about winning the championship, commit to the process of training like a champion.
- Or, like I did - instead of worrying about writing a best-selling book (the outcome), I

committed to the process of creating opportunities to share and publish my ideas on a consistent basis; initially through articles, workshops, conferences, and eventually, books. This book for example and the next one I'm writing.

- Instead of worrying about getting six-pack abs, commit to the process of eating healthy each day and exercising regularly. The outcome hopefully is going to be you feeling better and stronger, looking healthier and happier.

It's not just about the result; it's about discovering who you are and the **identity of the type of person you want to be** to be able to enjoy those results. This is step 1 and starts with sustainable, long-lasting change, not by focusing on results like your performance or your appearance. In the fixed mindset, this could become quite obsessive (fixed) and not attract change (growth).

As you have learned so far in this chapter, developing the right mindset is the first step, the crucial change that needs to happen to succeed.

...continuing my story on Mindset change.

As I refer back to my own story from Chapter 2 on values, particularly core values, when I was searching for that 'golden ticket', the ultimate senior position. Looking back on that experience now, as mentioned, I can clearly see why I applied for it, and accepted it, when I already had recently acquired a senior position that I had been striving towards for years. It was because I had a fixed mindset. I was running patterns in my mind to keep looking, to keep outdoing what I had achieved, but for what purpose. Because, in my mind I wanted more. I had achieved my first goal, I thought, and rather than adapting a growth mindset and applying my ideas, passions, and insights for the long term to that position, in my mind it was "well I've achieved what I never thought I could, it's been a long road, but maybe the grass is greener." Without any consideration of celebrating and applying my skills to what I had achieved I kept looking. I am sure you have also seen many people in this fixed mindset that need to *stop to smell the roses,* enjoy the moment, do what they love and have achieved for a while, then whilst embracing a growth mindset reflect and decide if, like in my story, there is any need to keep searching.

The position I was enjoying granted me much autonomy to create strategies and change to move the school forward; connecting with students and community members – ticking many of the boxes, so what was the purpose? Why was I stuck in this mindset for the 'ultimate post' to satisfy who I thought I was?

Once I got clarity on what were my core values or what motivated me, whilst in **a growth mindset**, things became clearer; I felt fresher, happier, as the coin had dropped, I had adapted my growth mindset to facilitate my own successful change on many levels, not just my career.

As frustrated as this situation made me at the time, it provided me with a valuable lesson because it gave me one of the final pieces in the puzzle.

What is a Mindset?

Your mindset is essentially the sum of your knowledge, including beliefs, values, and thoughts about the world and your place in it. It is your filter for the way you conduct your life – information you receive and information you give - the gatekeeper of how, and what you receive and how and why you react the way you do.

The mindset you adapt is used for a specific part in your life, as in "the mindset of an entrepreneur" or "the growth mindset." Having the right mindset for what you aim for is often the biggest factor for its success, or not, including your approach to any obstacles encountered along the way. Developing the right mindset is the way to learning something new, whilst extracting the most relevant information for your needs, helping you move towards what you want and achieving it. The filters you may put up in your mindset contribute to how and why you develop the beliefs that are most helpful for where you want to go or how you want to be. This belief-system is your mindset.

Generally, a good mindset will reflect your 'picture of the world,' your reality, and will help you. A starting point would be:

1. Find the beliefs that are most supportive of your goals and aims
2. Check if the beliefs are in harmony with your values, motivational drivers (see Chapters 2 and 3) and are a likely reality.

For example: creating a statement or affirmation towards a positive, committed goal or aspiration needs to have a 'likely reality.' Without consideration and focus on this, it is likely that your goal may not be achieved. Despite how carefully you word your goal or affirmation, and how convincing it may sound to you and your mindset, is it realistic? A simple illustration of a 'non-realistic' goal may be:

"In 7 days from now (insert date here) I will be twenty kilograms lighter and healthier." Maybe you will be, although it is very unrealistic to lose that much weight in a week, or if you do, you are likely to be unhealthy. It's a great goal to have, however in this example, be realistic around the time frame.

You have already moved towards creating a growth mindset in Chapter 4 with the C.R.E.A.T.E your Future process. Revisit the exercises and take another look.

The overall aim is that you want to use your mindset to make positive change. That's why your beliefs don't necessarily have to reflect your current reality. What you believe in, how committed you are to that belief and how you apply yourself to achieving that belief will determine your success. For example, if you believe "I am a successful entrepreneur" and you think and act that way, it is more likely you will succeed, rather than if your mindset is "I want to be a successful entrepreneur." **I want**, rather than **I am**, is exactly as the statement reads a 'wanna be' mindset. Remember, your mindset doesn't distinguish between real and imagined, so it/you focuses on the NO – the I want rather than the I am. The game-changer from these thoughts towards successful and effective change are the keywords *'I am'* rather than *'I want.'* It's powerful because it changes your mindset in an instant and therefore how you behave and enables you to grow.

Your Mindset Change workout

We all have the ability to change our mindset – to change our core inner beliefs upon which we base our view of ourselves and of the world, but changing beliefs is not an easy thing to do. The challenge with changing beliefs is based on many influences such as negative pre-conditioning, a result of years of the wrong self-talk, verbal feedback from various places and people; maybe work bosses, or as a young person coping with school and all the complications it brings, such as changing friendship groups; that teacher (s) you had that just didn't quite work for you; difficulty in understanding a concept or problem; something you heard, saw, environmental or cultural influences to name a few. To create and determine a positive change; a growth mindset enables us to rapidly install new thought patterns and positive mindsets, based on proven success models.

Trust that you can change your mindset to work for you, not against you. This changing mindset is empowered by positive thinking. To achieve this, you need to be confident and committed to do what is needed to put yourself into the correct frame of mind to propel yourself into focused action, expecting successful outcomes. You will require energy to succeed; not just an outcome focus with no effort, idea, or plan to get there. This approach, when the universe seems to rush to us like we are a magnet to assist us with our intended result, some may say is the phenomenon known as 'The Law of Attraction.' Mindset can be the difference that makes the difference.

Start at the beginning - *Mindset Fundamentals*

Step 1: Self Confidence and belief in yourself

We have all seen the research, heard the interviews and testimonies of people that continue to state "If you lack belief in yourself and in your capabilities, your self-esteem suffers." Reflect on this, believe it and embrace it as Step 1 towards developing a growth mindset. Without this, you are beaten in many ways before you start. You must identify that without believing in yourself and your goals, whatever you are striving towards; your ability to change your mindset, may be a long and difficult road to achievement. This is because negative thoughts around your self-esteem will often come by and spoil things, which further affects your self-confidence. This can result in a sense of worthlessness, helplessness and even hopelessness, which makes you feel inadequate and see everything as pointless. Then you counter your success by losing your motivation, your drive; there is no point , you are defeated before you begin. This is your state of mind to commit to changing what you need to, to get what you want. Achieve this and success for you is already happening. You have reached the outcome of Step 1 – achieving and 'being' confident in yourself. Congratulations! Accomplishing your goals and objectives becomes much easier because you are **empowered from the inside out.** You are **focused and in control**! You are **in charge**!

YOU CHOOSE to be a floating balloon spiraling upwards towards the rainbow of achievement and success, rather than a balloon constantly running out of fuel; losing focus and spiraling down towards the ground, with nowhere else left to go, except to hit the ground hard and start again, or not? Wouldn't you rather be floating up and up towards what you want, in a positive, self-confident state of mind, with the 'world at your feet' to choose your path, your journey, and, ultimately, YOUR SUCCESS.

Step 2: Determination & Perseverance

A major element of a positive mindset, focused on fulfilment of your goals and success, is developing determination and perseverance to overcome failures when they happen, and they will happen. The 'game changer' in continuing to remain focused and achieving your success is the reaction, meanings, and how you embrace those failures – how you deal with them. Do you succumb to them, get angry with them, or fight them in your mind? For example, if you consider a failure as meaning, you have wasted your time and react by giving up then how would you ever know your true potential; how would you ever know if you could achieve your success? Failure is to teach us. The process and journey to get there, however, may take some creative tweaking as it is hard sometimes.

The most important learning in this example is knowing the difference between keeping your focus and being creative to reflect and look at things differently, rather than simply 'giving up', and *being like that balloon*! A valuable skill is to be able to analyse and evaluate what went wrong and why. It is a reminder that very few things worth having are very easily attained! A growth mindset is conscious of the fact that one failure is not the end of the story but just one way it didn't work.

How accurate this statement is "True failure only

comes when we stop trying altogether."

Learning to ride a bicycle for the first time:

Remember that friend of yours, or maybe it was you, that was so excited to wake up early Christmas morning before dawn. How you had planned it all out for days and weeks before. How you were going to push back the sheets and blankets as quietly as you could, so not disturb even the noisiest of birds perched outside your window.

How you were going to put your socks on, so not to make a noise so you could carefully and quietly sneak down the hallway of your house from your bedroom, without being heard.

Your bedroom on Christmas morning always seemed a long way from the living room, where you knew the gifts would be. Most importantly where your sparkling, beautiful new bicycle was going to be. Your pride and joy. You had pictured the exact place it would be. You'd measured up the living room meticulously when nobody was home one afternoon. You'd worked out the only place your new bike would fit, amongst the furniture, the Christmas tree, and where any other gifts would likely be.

You were in an incredible state of excitement, happiness, nervousness, all at once. You were in an incredibly positive and creative mindset. You could probably take on any issue and easily 'knock it out of the park" right now. Life is great!

As you approached the living room, bonus, you weren't caught out by your parents - there it was, sparkling and glowing like a lighthouse on the cliff above the ocean, above fear. You were the happiest person in the world. So happy you could scream, yell, maybe cry or laugh. It didn't matter.

You kept that mindset, that positive, focused state of mind all day as you celebrated, and waited for a chance to actually sit on it and ride it. You were going to ride a bicycle for the first time.

It was nearly 'that time.' The time when your dad was going to take you outside with your new bike and teach you how to ride it. Wow, you were so excited you could 'pop'. However, like a storm approaching that lighthouse, you started having second thoughts. Part of you wanted to leave the bicycle right where it was, all shining and new, in its stunning majestic blue, just standing there in its pride of place. What shall you do, why are you thinking like this? Where is that focused mindset going - come on, bring it back to your goal, why you thought you wanted the bike in the first place?

The time had come and to follow your goal, you had to move the bicycle from its 'shiny podium' and take it outside and - ride it.

You and your dad carefully and with so much respect picked up your amazing new friend and took it outside to find that perfect place, that first contact it would have with the ground and your first time sitting on it and 'riding'.

After concentrating on instructions from your dad, with a large audience, you and your positive mindset and 'King of the World' state managed to climb up and sit on the soft leather seat for the first time. "Woohoo, look at me."

The question was asked from your parents; the permission you thought you had been waiting for, what seemed to you forever entered your consciousness like a wave crashing the rocks below your 'sparkling lighthouse'. "Are you ready to ride?"

Your 'glowing light of energy' that had been shining through your mind like a lightning bolt, started to fade. Why? Sitting up on the seat dad let go and you felt like you were starting to fall. Surely all you had to do was to hold on and push the pedals. You froze and the next thing you remember was hitting the ground - thud! It seemed like you had fallen through a deep rocky crevasse; were you on your way to Alice's house - with no white rabbit to guide you. The tears started to flow. "I can't do this," you screamed.

Calming words from your parents: "Up you get and try again." Huh? Try again, why. You planned this moment, it was engraved on your mind forever but it didn't work so why would you try it again? Your lighthouse had nearly gone out; you were mad, so mad. "How will I ever be able to ride a bike; this is not for me," your self-talk started yelling at you. Your state was changing rapidly. Your mindset was becoming fixed, and your 'balloon' was plummeting towards the ground. You believed you had failed, but another little voice in your head is pushing you and saying, "Come on try again" - you what?

To give it another go you take your mindset back to how you have felt all those months, days, yesterday, last night, this morning and up until a little while ago. You start to recall those thoughts, the positive, amazing way you felt. Why you wanted the bicycle - you goal was to that you wanted a bike to ride it, to soar through town, 'King of the World" - you said.

You have two choices, don't you?

Find the beliefs that are most supportive of your goals, aims, and achieving what you want.

Check if the beliefs are in harmony with your values, motivational drivers, and are a likely reality.

You change your mindset, your state, get back on the bike, focus on your goals, concentrate on your purpose, reflect on your passions and try over and over again until you can do it, you can achieve your goals. You are still a star. Well done. Be determined and persevere.

Step 3: Mindset and Action

As you can see so far in this chapter and referring to previous chapters, particularly on values, beliefs and motivational drivers, the correct positive and growth mindset leads to proactive, rather than reactive positive actions towards outcomes. Even when you are unsure or unable to proceed because of lack of knowledge or skill, adapting a positive, growth mindset enables you to approach, research, and acquire those skill sets, until you are able to achieve the actions you already know will be necessary to succeed. Your core inner beliefs and thought patterns are what leads to your feelings of potentiality, action, and achieving the results you desire.

One element that can and will get in your way to achieving success; to having a growth, rather than fixed mindset, is what you say to yourself – your Self talk.

Your Self Talk - friend and foe. You need to listen, monitor and change it. How? Pay attention to your thoughts as you will likely discover that you are processing a lot of negative self-talk. Discovering this can be frustrating and irritating at first. You may feel powerless to make the changes you want, or create anxious feelings of uncertainty, perceiving you have no control over the thoughts that are driving you, or are flooding your mind and your life, generating more negative self-talk, and so the circle continues. As a start, acknowledge an awareness of a few of those negative patterns of thought and commit to begin your process to change them into positive thoughts, using the tools presented here and in previous chapters. You will feel much happier, purpose-driven, content, stronger, and more in control, rather than always seeming that you are "chasing your dragon's tail."

It is as simple as starting to flip your mindset through using positive statements to help you create the changes you want. Commit to start, and enjoy the experiences, the changes that will follow and the positive benefits that using this initial simple technique will deliver.

When you commit to change, use language, particularly in your self-talk to focus on what you want, your positive state, rather than a negative or 'away from – what you don't want.' Monitor this; be in charge of what thoughts you allow to flow through your mind. This initial process puts you in charge of creating your 'world' the way you want it. Firstly, you internalize it using tools as allies, rather than problems – such as positive self-talk; maintaining focus on the changes you want; keeping motivated towards success rather than allowing yourself to submit to an away from motivation, or negative self-talk - creating your world the way you want it internally. Later you will confidently apply these tools externally and attract the success you want.

It is often hard for people to imagine and accept that they are planning their journey. Instead of allowing your unconscious mind to be in charge, step up, take charge. Direct YOUR thoughts to show that YOU ARE IN CONTROL and you are the sensible confident and committed leader of you, steering the direction of where you want to go.

Imagine you are the Captain of the ship, but your crew (your mindset) sails the ship. It is always up to you to create the change, then draw upon your 'crew', your 'tools', your allies to DO it. Only YOU can make YOU DO IT!

Take Action - Changing Your Mindset

The following can help you to develop the right mindset for your situation:

Step 4: Source only the best Information:

Depending on what it is you want to change, identify sources that will provide for you the best information in that field. Then focus on learning this information only. Be decisive, committed, and focus the specific information you want to learn and input to your mindset that will be the most effective. Keep focused on your aims and the success you want.

Step 5: Role Model the Best People:

Similar to Step 4, look for the best people in the area you are researching or focused on and try to model what they do, how they do it and why they do what they do. Associate to them, daydream a bit to imagine you are them and adopt their kind of thinking and mindset. Follow them. You can get plenty of information about how they are thinking, their advice, what they did from sources such as auto- biographies, available memoirs, newsreels, videos and posts they have made about certain things. See these, read these, and start to identify with traits they have that may be similar to yours, or that you want to have in order to achieve your growth mindset, be confident, and achieve your goals.

A famous saying by entrepreneur, author, and motivational speaker Jim Rohn is: "*You're the average of the five people you spend the most time with*". Also, "*Show me your friends and I'll show you your future.*" Hard words, but if you think about them, it does make sense. Notice the people around you. Who do you socialize with, lunch with, speak about work or relationships with? To assist you in your goals, make sure that you're spending time with people who are in line with **what you want for your own life** (preferably people "better" than you so it raises your average). It's compelling and it's provocative. More discussion on *modelling* as a process to success is discussed in the next chapter.

Step 6: Examine Your Current Beliefs:
What are your beliefs around certain issues, particularly the issues you want to positively change in your mindset? Explore your mindset by looking at your current belief-system. Are these beliefs supporting you? Or are there self-limiting beliefs? You have to identify those possible blocks and turn them around, because whether you know about limiting beliefs or not, they are working in your subconscious mind, driving you towards or away from the success you strive for.

To uncover and discover your beliefs, ask yourself the

right questions about where you want to go and what is standing in your way right now; tools we have already seen throughout this book the key is to turn those beliefs around by declaring supportive statements on the same belief.

Step 7: Shape Your Mindset with Vision and Goals

Be proactive in building your mindset. Establish clearly where you want to go, what you want to achieve, and most importantly why you want to achieve 'it'. Having a clear vision, pictures, and sounds describing your end result clearly in your mind's eye, will create a strong pull towards this end result, because you can see yourself achieving it and feel yourself experiencing it – associating your mind into the experience that you want. Get excited!

Step 8: Listen to Your Inner Voice

One of the most wonderful things is when from listening to your inner voice and changing your mindset, you keep focused on what you want, your success, your aims and not what you don't want, you find your very own way, YOUR voice.

An old Cherokee told his grandson, *"My son, there is a battle between two wolves inside us all. One is Evil. It is anger, jealousy, greed, resentment, inferiority, lies, and ego. The other is Good. It is joy, peace, love, hope, humility, kindness, empathy, and truth." The boy thought about it, and asked, "Grandfather, which wolf wins?" The old man quietly replied, "The one you feed."* -Author Unknown

This is a great illustration of finding your voice, and

keeping your focus. You are gifted with an inner "knowingness." By developing and building a relationship of trust with your voice, it can lead you to an empowered life filled with amazing outcomes and achievement of your goals and desires. Listen, begin to pay attention, and you will slowly begin to hear the different voices or "wolves" within you, and the choice will become yours as to which one you will feed.

Try it!

Try this activity right now. Grab a sheet of paper, a pen, find a quiet space, relax, and listen to your 'inner voice'. Now in a relaxed state ask yourself and note the answers you receive. 'Ask the universe, your inner mind, and you shall receive." Don't think about them too much, or spend too long on creating a response. Just note down your initial thoughts.

7 questions for 7 solutions for success

- What are YOU good at? (Mind)
- What do YOU love doing? (Heart)
- What need can YOU serve? (Body)
- What is life asking of YOU?
- What gives YOU life meaning and purpose?
- What do YOU want to be doing?
- What is YOUR conscience directing you to do? (Spirit)

Listening to your voice, and asking yourself questions with 100% honesty and authenticity is the unique thing that you can add to the world, because it's who you are. This is a sure way to achieve your success, your goals, and moreover to develop a success mindset - forever to add to your confidence, your motivation and to your life pursuits. Look and ask your inner self to help you to find what and who you really are.

Step 9: Protect your Mindset

As is life, you will come across obstacles to your success, naysayers, non-supporters, people, and things that want to drag you down. This will cause you overwhelm, frustration, sadness and disappointments along the way, protect your mindset – protect YOU. Keeping your focus and your confidence is the changemaker to maintaining and developing success. You will be fine if you remember that.

Summary: 10 keys for living your success from the inside out

1. Define your success: Number 1. What do you want? Why do you want it? Be clear on these goals. Define them, or you will remain confused about your success and be preoccupied about your failures. Find out what's important for you in various aspects of your life.

2. Set your goals based on your definition: Assume that right now, you are at a stage where you think you know what success means to you, but you have no plan, no help, nor any strategy to live that success. Unpack the how! Start by setting goals in the three basic areas of life: work, relationships, and health.

3. Find inspiration and motivation: Setting goals is just the start, not the end. The next step is for you to find a way, examples, models to convince your brain to stick to your goals and become inspired about how to move ahead. Find some ways to intrinsically motivate yourself –

4. Create habits surrounding and towards achieving your goals: Goal-setting works best when you have habits surrounding your goal. Your habits are directly related to the rate of depletion of your motivation levels, so if you're not habitual about doing things that are needed for achieving your goals, your motivation levels will deplete more quickly.

5. Create routines around your habits: There is no doubt that successful people have this noticeable thing in their lives: they live their success, whether anyone notices them or not. Learn to accept, nurture and live your success. Do the best work you want to end up with today; commit yourself to the toughest of tasks.

6. Stop procrastinating: Routines can be a pain and get 'old' quickly. Even the most successful people will time lapse because of their habit of procrastinating. There will be times when inspiration will stop flowing and life will seem pointless; you will feel defeated and your time will get wasted. Here, the best advice would be to go back to Step 3, because this is the time when you need motivation and inspiration the most.

7. Don't look at success like a distant achievement: "I

wish I was that successful." "When will I reach that success?" Stop considering success from a point of view where success is different from you as an individual, and is merely something you hope to attain one day.

8. Be willing to change: You own your thoughts. You are your thoughts, so You can change them. Although your beliefs most likely formed when you were young from different sources, you still have the power to affect change in your life. This is the essence of personal power: choice and responsibility.

9. Feed the Mindset you want: It makes sense that the fastest, most effective way to change your mindset is to 'feed' your mind with what you want. Remember, every time you 'feed' yourself a positive message, a positive mindset with focused instructions, it weakens and prevents the negative ones. You will be instantly creating new neurons that form a new, more positive neural network. Therefore, the more you do this the stronger your new neural network will become. Attracting the positive and feeding the positive weakens the negative.

10. Create passion for your Mindset: Allow yourself to create a passion for your new and changing Mindset. Be consistent with this to create endorphins in your body that enable you to feel better, happier – feel a new sense of well-being. Naturally, you will likely therefore feel more inspired, emotionally engaged, have more fun in your life, more success as you grow and make stronger your neural network.

Start Today – 10-minute daily process for success

After I learned this, I have always felt happy and inspired to do more. Instead of searching for some distant success, search for success in your day-to-day life—find success with the smallest bits of work that help you reach your goal. Then stay committed to those habits and strive to live them daily. I find that successful people live by these rules; they don't really search for success. Instead *they set these habitual routines into their lives*, consciously or unconsciously, and seek out the best way forward. Now you know it, it's your time to make you happen the way you want to live; change yourself. Consciously create habits that improve your life, and learn to live successfully with them. Pick one thing you want to change NOW. It could be anything – a belief, an attitude to something, solving a problem – something you want instead.

Imagine what you want – close your eyes, create a huge smile on your face and allow your imagination to run wild for a moment. Embrace any resistance – it's ok, just your old neural network testing you again.

Using the power of your imagination, trust it to vividly picture what you really want. Take yourself there, feel any emotion, listen to any sounds around you- while you are there – where you want to be – having what you want. Yes, that's right, you are there. Confidently step into the moment, into the picture. Imagine the colours more vivid, the volume around you clear and precise, the smells just how you imagined them. You are in the moment. Stay there for a moment, enjoy it.

Now slowly and gradually accept all that you have just

experienced, keep the smile on your face and gradually open your eyes, back to now. Feeling great, feeling fulfilled and happy.

Mentally rehearse this – do this – for 10 minutes a day. Strengthen it by adding energy, enthusiasm, inspiration, happiness, and fun.

Before long, you will be taking small actions that will reinforce your new mindset, your new success.

Read on for the final chase– Modelling.

Chapter 8
Be Your Dragon! – Modelling

"The reason I see so far is because I stand on the tall shoulders of those who came before me" - Sir Isaac Newton

What is modelling?

Modelling is the process of recreating excellence. We can model any human behavior by mastering the beliefs, the physiology and the specific thought processes (that is the strategies) that underlie the skill or behavior. It is about achieving an outcome by studying how someone else goes about it.

Modelling is something you have been doing your whole life, but its's likely you have not been aware of it. Most people model randomly and unselectively. That is, without conscious awareness. Modelling is a specific tool that, when fully applied can propel you towards tremendous success. For example, Oprah Winfrey is quoted as saying *"When I did my first audition for my first television job, I was such a nervous wreck. I had no idea what to do or say. I thought that maybe I'll pretend I'm Barbara Walters. I will sit like Barbara and hold my head like Barbara. I crossed my legs at the ankles, like Barbara, I put my little finger under my chin, I leaned across the desk and I pretended I was Barbara Walters."*

At its core, modelling is selecting a person you admire, studying the methodology behind their success and creating a similar path for yourself. This technique is one of the best keys to being successful, and can be successfully deployed in almost every aspect of your life. Basically,

Modelling is the process of recreating, replicating excellence and Installing it in individuals, groups and organisations. We can model any human behaviour by mastering the beliefs the physiology and the specific thought processes (the strategies) that underlie the skill or behaviour. It is about achieving an outcome by studying how someone else goes about it. The test for modelling success is – Show them how to do it. Can they do it?

Indicators that you may have done modelling before are, for example, you may have taken on a number of activities, traits, the physiology, and embarked on focused study of a person you, at some level, wanted to 'be like', or moreover wanted to have some of their traits in your own personal life, career or finances, to name a few.

This may not have actually been a 'modelling process' but absolutely, was most certainly an

expression of your positive intentions to attempt to follow in the footsteps of one or two people that inspired you, who you admired and wanted to 'be like'.

This could have occurred when you were a young child at school, with an admiration for a fellow student, a sportsman, a teacher, or a musician, for example that you looked up to, or aspired to be?

This is known as *Modelling.* Modelling is closely linked to all you have read in this book so far, particularly the last chapter on 'Mindset'. Modelling is the science of you creating your own change. For example, you may want to be more like Richard Branson in business and marketing. Modelling works through a process of association and study of everything about that person related to the aspects of the person you want to be like and the way you conduct, for example marketing and business. You can start to conduct that area in your own business positively differently and reap the rewards.

Where does modelling come from?

The history of the idea of *modelling*, often referred to as the 'Science of Achievement" started in the 1970's with Richard Bandler and Frank Pucelik modelling Fritz Perls a gestalt therapist.* Richard Bandler is an American author and trainer in the field of self-help, best known as the co-creator, with John Grinder of Neuro-linguistic pro-gramming (NLP). NLP is basically a methodology to understand and change human behaviour patterns. The concept of the ability to *model* somebody came from Bandler helping a university colleague, Robert Spitzer edit *The Gestalt Approach* (1973) based on a manuscript by Fritz Perls. According to Spitzer, Bandler came out of it talking and acting like Fritz Perls, and so the idea of learning another's behaviour and applying it to your own goals and aspirations was born. The idea being that it is possible to rapidly and unconsciously assimilate complex patterns of genius and then display them in your own behavior.

(*According to *Psychology Today* magazine, Gestalt therapy is a client-centered approach to psychotherapy that helps clients focus on the present and understand what is really happening in their lives right now, rather than what they may perceive to be happening based on past experience.)

Learning to walk – Modelling

This theory of modelling shouldn't come as a surprise to you. For example, when you watch a child take its first steps, there likely has not been any verbal instructions, teaching the child how to walk. Remembering, an infant child that young, when learning to walk, has minimal to no verbal language acquisition, nor understanding of the functions of weight distribution, muscle memory, concept of getting onto their legs. Yet somehow, from their own pre-verbal analysis, is able to walk from A to B, into your smiling arms and excited squeals of praise and conversation. Ok, that's an extreme description – but is it really? Literally this is how you learn as you get older- is it not?

As a student, we are given verbal instructions and explanations at school on how to do things. Learning to ride a bicycle your parents likely through spoken instructions and demonstration show you how to sit on a bicycle without it falling over; how you need to hold the handle bars to keep balanced, and place both feet on the pedals, push the pedals; whilst distributing your weight across the seat and so on, so as not to fall. The point being so much of how you learn is traditionally reliant on language as a way of knowing; a way of learning. As you do rely on instructions and verbal information about how to do things you forget that as an infant you had none of this.

As an infant you learnt through copying, observing, processing at an unconscious level with the aim to assimilate. For example, your parents may have beckoned you to come to them, so from modelling what you saw around you, you taught yourself; you learned how to get from floor to your parents – crawling, then walking. You modeled what you wanted to achieve. As a pre- verbal child, you have the ability to assimilate unconsciously without any understanding. The outcome being that within the assimilation process you learned and developed complex patterns of behavior, language and other things that were available in your surrounding environment

What's the model for modelling? Steps in understanding and modelling behaviour for your success

Step 1: A model of modelling essentially is to study a person whom you want to be like yourself, in various or in particular aspects of your life. Look for someone who is already successful in your chosen field, or someone who has created the kind of life you want to live. Look into their history and their rise to the top. How did they get to where they are today? What kind of obstacles and setbacks did they face, and how did they overcome them? What are their philosophies about their life and their work? Use this information to build a path that mirrors theirs.

For example, you may be inspired in business to be like Richard Branson, have his success, have his 'genius'. I say genius as often in a model of modelling the concept of "Find a genius; study that genius in every way; learn how to be 'that' person in the chosen area of your life that your 'genius' inspires you, so the aspects of what inspires you, you want to 'model' and incorporate into your own life."

However, you can easily get caught up in the 'hype of genius' and become quite obsessed with the celebrity status of your chosen genius, which in your mind, will always be beyond your reach. Therefore, you will always be 'trying to be like that person'. A play on words, but you understand that if you believe you are always 'trying' and can never be like that person anyway the modelling process will not work, as you have already decided it is beyond your reach.

The idea of genius: Be careful about this idea of 'genius'. Genius is not and does not necessarily need to be confined to well-known so-called 'celebrities of genius'. There are elements of genius in everyone. You and 'everyone' do have things that you do which are brilliant. You will find if you open your eyes and ears in your everyday life you will see examples of genius that may attract you. It may be the way a colleague ran a meeting; an insightful, inspiring conversation you witnessed between your child and his or her teacher; a Speaker that had great energy that engaged and inspired you throughout. The examples are endless. Modelling may be that from those examples perhaps you want to adapt some specific skills to 'be the same'; 'have the same confidence'; be able to inspire people from your presentations or speaking and so on. Your aim is to 'model' those chosen behaviours, associate and assimilate with them yourself for your own development, or improvement? While the people around you may not be 'geniuses' in every context or aspect of their performance, there are things they do which are absolutely superb.

Genius presents itself big and bold and also small and subtle. You don't want to overlook the small as they may be excellent targets of opportunity for you to find example of genius. It may be your next-door neighbor; it may be your spouse; it may be your child and yes, it may be someone extremely famous. After you've succeeded in identifying a genius and gaining access to this genius, it is important to remind yourself of the why? That is, what is the context in which they're behaving as a genius that you want to be and have in your life. This is an important step as you go into the next stage of *modelling*.

Step 2: the second step is the unconscious assimilation of specific patterns of behaviour, with clear purpose that you are modelling. That is, it is highly likely that you don't want to assimilate patterns in all the contexts in which you could have access to such a genius. Rather, modelling the patterns for your purpose, for your success; in the particular areas that you want to associate with and assimilate into your life.

Let me speak personally. When I first had opportunities in public speaking, I was excited, energized and confident, however I wanted to be the best I could be. My role as a Speaker is to not just speak. It has many elements such as my appearance, physiology – how I come across to the audience, how to engage the people in the room, how to use the stage space well, without walking backwards and forwards every few seconds. I'm sure we've all seen speakers like this that make us dizzy trying to follow them. Then it was the actual speaking part. How do I speak, how to use silence as a tool in speaking, pacing and leading what I'm speaking about, rapport with the audience, sometimes referred to as 'reading the room'. If I'm using technology how does it look, is it too text heavy, is it visually engaging and so on. Many elements directly related to speaking successfully, or not.

Being in education and teaching, I had seen many speakers and teachers. As a teacher, I adjusted and learnt about my own speaking and developed that as I became a

Speaker and facilitating workshops at conferences, for example. Like I said, I was confident and a good speaker, according to my audiences and workshop participants. However, I wanted to be even better, more engaging and entertaining, so I started to watch and learn from speakers that inspired me. I decided that if was going to step up my game I needed to observe and learn from the best. I set my goal; my ultimate test as a speaker, to be selected and to give a TED talk. I pictured myself in the middle of the stage on the round red carpet delivering an awesome talk. I started modelling great speakers. The way they stood, how they worked the audience and used the stage. How they used their voice. Their physiological traits, use of language, what clothing and colours that they wore. How they used silence, techniques to engage the audience and keep them engaged and so on. I used the process of modelling the best, to be the best. From all this observing and research, I was drawn to one particular speaker. I decided and wanted his absolute patterns of genius in his ability to communicate directly, engage, excite, energize with people in the room. I modelled these aspects of his behaviour as a speaker and very quickly 'became him' on stage in many ways. My speaking process improved exponentially and yes, I got to give that TED talk and other keynote speaking opportunities and continue to enjoy them.

From the person or people, you want to model, you appreciate that there are other aspects of their personal character; the other aspects and traits in their life. It is important to segment the contexts to the behaviours that you want, and be very clear why you want them. If you're going to put yourself in a position of unconsciously assimilating, as you did with your parents and the patterns which they presented; make sure that you do this only in contexts where there are patterns of genius available so you don't assimilate elements which would not be useful for you in any sense.

The basic elements in modelling

There are basically three broad approaches to modelling. The first one is:

> **1. Imitation**
> a. Identify the person you want to model. Find someone or someone's behaviour that is worth modelling. Specifically, the aspects of that person that you want to 'install' in yourself. Be clear on the why. Without clarity on the why, the possibility of you being successful will be very limited.
> b. Study and work on copying those behaviours, and incorporating them into your own life.

The second approach is more detailed and is the:

> **2. Cognitive approach**
> a. *Analyse the components* that you want to model, and why?
> b. Study the *physiology* of those behaviours and aspects.
> c. Research and decide on the *strategies* the person you are modelling are using, in reference always, to the traits or elements you want to model and 'install' in yourself.
> d. Research to understand what is the *motivation* of the person you are modelling, why they behave the way they do. How they do what it is about them

that you want to include in your life.

e. *Contrastive Analysis.* This is when you analyse yourself in the context of what you are currently doing compared to the person you are modelling. This self-analysis separates what is essential from idiosyncratic. That is what is the difference that makes the difference. Then consciously and purposefully start breaking things down to find what is essential for you to succeed.

f. *Sensitivity Analysis.* This important self-reflective process is for you to determine what is critical. This is an important call to action for you to start changing things to find out if they make any difference. To find out if the changes make a difference to you in terms of the results you achieve.

g. *Internal Strategies.* From the previous analytical and comparative steps, you aim to find out what are they doing 'in their heads' while they do it. It sounds a little cryptic, but the point of this step is to go beyond copying and to identify how they think when they are doing what it is you want to do to be successful.

h. Explore the *power of change* by associating into all this cognitive work you have done to be like that person, or 'be that person' in the area that you want to change.

The third approach, and maybe the easiest is to ask somebody who is already successful doing what it is you want.

3. Ask for help

No matter what it is you're after, someone is already doing it. If it's someone you already know or have a connection to, so much the better. You don't just have to study them from afar to learn how they found the key to success; you can ask them to share their experiences with you, and perhaps guide you along the path to your own achievements. You may also consider hiring a Results Coach to help you.

Postlude
Dragon's Flight– Soar to Success

"People who soar are those who refuse to sit back, sigh and wish things would change. They neither complain of their lot nor passively dream of some distant ship coming in. Rather, they visualize in their minds that they are not quitters; they will not allow life's circumstances to push them down and hold them under." - Charles R. Swindoll

One thing can change everything. One event, one thought, one act of kindness, one act of violence, one moment can change everything. Even this book could be your one thing that causes you to choose differently. Remember it is not the events in our lives that determine our destiny, but what we decide about those events. Deciding to turn your dreams into realities and finding passion in your purpose is the very first step in accomplishing just that.

We are each given our own individual universe to shape as we will. We are constantly shaping our universe all the time, either consciously or unconsciously. Every thought we have, every word we utter, every action we take communicates something to the universe around us and sculpts it in some way. By practicing and learning the skills taught in this book, you empower yourself to take conscious control of the tools that define your world each and every moment of your life. This book is not meant to be read one time through, but rather to be a reference and guidebook to be revisited over and over again either in its entirety or particular chapters or topics which you want to further clarify or read again.

Remember that you now have the power to strategically see, hear, feel, and create your future, then literally carve it out in the way you choose. You now have the power and knowledge to win the game of life in the way you want to see it play out.

The people who are able to produce the most in terms of results are those who have the ability to enlist the cooperation of others to assist them in accomplishing their objectives. By mastering your interpersonal communication skills as well as your ability to influence, you are empowered to produce extraordinary results.

You have the capacity to master all that is contained in this book. Use the tools to expand your rule book and reach outward with new strategies and skill sets to gain understanding and proficiency in new areas. Break through the boundary conditions of your current thinking to embrace all that is possible for you! By doing that, you will forge opportunities you never thought possible and the playing field of your game will encompass so much more than you previously allowed.

I know how much this knowledge changed my life and the lives all those who I have taught. If you would like to join me and learn more about what is possible for you, and would like to drop me a line, please do. I would enjoy following your continued journey. I can be reached via craig@craigfullerton.com.au. For more insights, ideas, and opportunities to work together, please visit my website via www.craigfullerton.com.au.

I would like to thank you for having faith in me and making the choice to buy this book. I hope I have in some way inspired you to strive for your greatest aspirations in your personal and professional life, knowing that with these tools you can achieve your greatest aspirations. Be happy and most of all learn to believe in yourself and your ability to create a magical reality- because reality is only what you choose it to be. As you take these skills and go along your way with passion and purpose, I ask that you take care, dream big, and make each day an extraordinary adventure.

Thank you and warmest wishes,
Craig Fullerton

LEARN FROM THE AUTHOR!
SPECIAL OFFERS AS THANK YOU FOR YOUR TRUST

1. DRAGON COACHING PACKAGE

Most people enroll in this program because they want to learn how to unleash their true potential by improving their thought patterns and get more from their lives. Most, quickly realise the power of these tools and insights and implement them in their life and celebrate their results. Complimentary initial session followed by opportunities for further sessions and programs with significant discounts and bonuses.

2. MENTORING AND COACHING PACKAGE

Maybe you are an aspiring leader, or looking for ways to accelerate your career - this program delivers. You will learn how to dramatically improve your thinking using the most revolutionary neuro-psychological tools available today. You will discover how your mind really works and gain quick, practical tools that hold the power to achieve your goals and turn your life around. Following a complimentary personal session, you will have the opportunity to explore a significantly discounted program with materials and follow up.

1. 'THE WAY FORWARD' – CV / COLLEGE PREP PACKAGE

This is student and job-seeker focused and teaches you tools for success in moving forward with your career, your future. You will explore and experience tools and techniques such as - How to interview, what to put in a CV, what it should look like and why. How to present yourself as unique; identify your points of difference that recruiters want to see. Following an initial meeting to determine your 'map', what you will learn to understand and cover in this package you will be prepared for life.

4. DRAGON GROUP COACHING
FOR YOUR TEAM

An executive package of coaching including leadership coaching. You and your team will receive the support, tools, and coaching to achieve sustained behavioral change. A unique element of my coaching methodology includes current neurological research which will further help members of your team to embrace behavioral change, implement and maintain new skillsets and support for optimum performance. Following a complementary introductory session, opportunities for a personal discounted program catered for you including materials and follow up.

5. 'GET STARTED- VIP PACKAGE'

Aspiring Leadership coaching and mentor session for you to determine where you are, where you want to be, why you want to be there, and how to get there. This session will include an audit of your current CV and guidelines for preparation of a new CV and format for letters of application as you celebrate your new 'leadership' self. Complimentary session and heavily reduced program opportunities to pursue.

ABOUT ATMOSPHERE PRESS

Atmosphere Press is an independent, full-service publisher for excellent books in all genres and for all audiences. Learn more about what we do at atmospherepress.com.

We encourage you to check out some of Atmosphere's latest releases, which are available at Amazon.com and via order from your local bookstore:

Disruption Games: How to Thrive on Serial Failure, nonfiction by Trond Undheim

Itsuki, a novel by Zach MacDonald

A Surprising Measure of Subliminal Sadness, short stories by Sue Powers

Eyeless Mind, nonfiction by Stephanie Duesing

Saint Lazarus Day, short stories by R. Conrad Speer

My Father's Eyes, a novel by Michael Osborne

The Lower Canyons, a novel by John Manuel

A Blameless Walk, nonfiction by Charles Hopkins

The Horror of 1888, nonfiction by Betty Plombon

Shiftless, a novel by Anthony C. Murphy

White Snake Diary, nonfiction by Jane P. Perry

From Rags to Rags, essays by Ellie Guzman

The Escapist, a novel by Karahn Washington

A Cage Called Freedom, a novel by Paul P.S. Berg

Giving Up the Ghost, essays by Tina Cabrera

Family Legends, Family Lies, nonfiction by Wendy Hoke

Shining in Infinity, a novel by Charles McIntyre

Buildings Without Murders, a novel by Dan Gutstein

ABOUT THE AUTHOR

Craig Fullerton is considered an inspirational thought leader in integral education, an engaging storyteller, author, inspirational Coach, and international TED and keynote speaker, committed to sharing his research for innovation in education.

He is committed to empowering students and professionals to perform at peak levels for a vision-driven, transformative impact. By opening up challenging and transparent conversations, whether in an education or coaching environment, he is able to lead people of all ages and vocations to uncover their motivational drivers, needs and values to create and sustain meaningful change and cultivate the leaders of tomorrow.

Ideas are based on a lifetime of research and insights on approaches to learning, coaching and mentoring, drawn from hands-on experience across multiple senior teaching, and leadership roles; personal and executive coaching.

Craig's approach is based on an *integral model* of learning that incorporates aspects of neuroscience, cognitive psychology, associative learning, and Neuro Linguistic Programming.

Craig holds advanced degrees in Educational Leadership and Management; is a certified NLP Master Coach and Trainer, Global Leaders of the Future 360 Assessor; and a Certified Executive Coach with Marshall Goldsmith Stakeholder Centered Coaching.

You can connect with Craig via craig@ craigfullerton.com.au and visit his website, www.craigfullerton.com.au.